Writing Ethnography

TEACHING WRITING

Volume 2

Series Editor

Patricia Leavy
USA

International Editorial Board

Liza Ann Acosta, *North Park University, USA*
Sandra L. Faulkner, *Bowling Green State University, USA*
Lee Gutkind, *Arizona State University, USA*
Anne Harris, *Monash University, Australia*
Yvonna S. Lincoln, *Texas A&M University, USA*
David Manderson, *University of West Scotland, UK*
Ronald Pelias, *Southern Illinois University, USA*
Rita Rud, *Washington State University, USA*
Candace Stout, *The Ohio State University, USA*
Jonathan Wyatt, *The University of Edinburgh, UK*

Scope

The *Teaching Writing* series publishes concise instructional writing guides. Series books each focus on a different subject area, discipline or type of writing. The books are intended to be used in undergraduate and graduate courses across the disciplines and can also be read by individual researchers or students engaged in thesis work.

Series authors must have a demonstrated publishing record and must hold a PhD, MFA or the equivalent. Please email queries to the series editor at pleavy7@aol.com

Writing Ethnography

Jessica Smartt Gullion
Texas Woman's University, USA

SENSE PUBLISHERS
ROTTERDAM/BOSTON/TAIPEI

A C.I.P. record for this book is available from the Library of Congress.

ISBN: 978-94-6300-379-7 (paperback)
ISBN: 978-94-6300-380-3 (hardback)
ISBN: 978-94-6300-381-0 (e-book)

Published by: Sense Publishers,
P.O. Box 21858,
3001 AW Rotterdam,
The Netherlands
https://www.sensepublishers.com/

All chapters in this book have undergone peer review.

Printed on acid-free paper

PRAISE FOR
WRITING ETHNOGRAPHY

"In this foundational text, Gullion accomplishes the herculean task of talking about the overlooked process of ethnographic writing with an intimate tone. It is like we are seated at her desk writing along with her. Gullion uses interesting exemplars and personal examples to show the important process of writing ethnography. This text will be required reading in my research methods courses and for my graduate students because of the meticulous breakdown of writing practice that creates a text that is both useful and engaging."
– Sandra Faulkner, PhD, Associate Professor of Communication, Bowling Green State University and author of *Family Stories, Poetry, and Women's Work* and *Poetry as Method: Reporting Research Through Verse*

"When we were in the playwriting program together at New York University, John Belluso (the brilliant queer playwright who pioneered 'crip theatre' in the United States, and who died far too young) and I used to go see every new show together. I'd push him home up 2nd Avenue on the East Side and we'd debrief the show we'd just seen. John's only criterion was ever: "Did she have something to say?" Jessica Smartt Gullion has something to say, and she says it, as always, in a smart (smart by name, smart by nature), readable, and useful way. I love this writer because she does her homework, cares about her readers, and writes a damn good story. Buy this book immediately."
– Anne Harris, PhD, Senior Lecturer of Education, Monash University and author of *Critical Plays: Embodied Research for Social Change* and *The Creative Turn: Toward a New Aesthetic Imaginary*

"The art of constructing writing from research in meaningful ways that engages readers to 'linger in the scene' awaits you in *Writing Ethnography*. As Jessica Smartt Gullion empowers you to provoke and incite social change, she does so in ways that diminish the complexities of producing public scholarship. I invite you to engage in this collaborative process aimed to healthfully enhance our craft, working to ensure that people who need our compelling stories receive them most optimally, so our efforts may favorably linger beyond words and pages."
– miroslav pavle manovski, PhD, independent scholar and author of *Arts-Based Research, Autoethnography, and Music Education: Singing Through a Culture of Marginalization*

"Jessica Smartt Gullion's book is "directed to graduate students and new researchers," yet I would urge experienced ethnographers to read and to use this book in your classrooms. Gullion quotes Norman Denzin's charge to qualitative researchers to write social science that matters, and Gullion has done that in spades."
– **Stacy Holman Jones, Professor, Centre for Theatre and Performance, Monash University and author of the *Handbook of Autoethnography,* with Tony E. Adams and *Autoethnography,* with Tony E. Adams and Carolyn Ellis**

"Gullion acts as a gentle guide as she opens up ways in which people could conceptualize and execute writing ethnographies. She writes in accessible language and argues for the importance of such intelligibility. She offers tanglible examples, creates possibilities, and shares her process of writing, publishing, and even working with rejection. This is a must read for anyone who is learning about ethnography and is unsure about how to start writing."
– **Kakali Bhattacharya, PhD, Associate Professor of Educational Leadership, Kansas State University**

"Jessica Smartt Guillon's new important book on ethnography is accessible and comprehensive. She carefully takes the reader through the nuts and bolts of ethnographic writing with clear examples of different narrative structures. The text is encouraging and filled with practical advice. Highly recommended for social science graduate students and qualitative research courses."
– **Kris Clark, Associate Professor of Social Work, Fresno State University**

"Gullion provides a comprehensive history of ethnography, describes essential aspects of ethnographic fieldwork, identifies rarely discussed issues such as writing, editing, and publishing ethnographic research and shows how (and why) contemporary ethnogaphers can (need to) create vulnerable, creative, evocative, and socially-just tales. This succinctly and accessible text will make a fine resource for both new and skilled ethnographers."
– **Tony E. Adams, Associate Professor of Communication, Northeastern Illinois University and author of *Narrating the Closet: An Autoethnography of Same-Sex Attraction* and co-editor of *On (Writing) Families***

TABLE OF CONTENTS

ACKNOWLEDGEMENTS

Before I published my first book, I'd read acknowledgements sections and wonder who all those people were and how they could have contributed to the final text. I discovered through my own publishing journey that while the act of writing is generally a solitary endeavor, we draw on our communities to move our work from idea to printed book.

This book never would have come to fruition had it not been for Patricia Leavy. Thank you for your big loans from the girl zone. I have been so blessed by your friendship and your support for my work. Thanks also to Peter de Liefde and the staff at Sense Publishers. Always a pleasure to work with you.

Dian Jordan Werhane, my cheerleader and friend. This book is dedicated to you. I'm looking forward to reading all of yours.

Thanks also to Anne Harris and miroslav manovski for your support and words of publishing wisdom. Anne, I'm delighted that you let me include your writing as an example of writing for social change. And much thanks and love to the rest of my ABR and ICQI friends. I'd also like to thank Amy Minton, whom I've only met online in a wonderful writing group called (appropriately) The Year I Finished the Book, for your suggestion to linger in the scenes. I use it often.

I am truly blessed to work at a university that supports and encourages my work. Thanks to my departmental and other colleagues at Texas Woman's University for your positive words. I would like to acknowledge the graduate students in my Fall 2014 Qualitative and Spring 2015 Advance Qualitative Methods courses, for listening to my ideas and helping to flesh them out. Particular thanks to Jessica Williams. Another thanks to Abigail Tilton, Gretchen Busl, Stacy Greathouse, and Sally Stabb for the Just Write sessions. I wrote a lot of this book during those.

Over my academic career, a number of people have taken the time to mentor me as a writer. Brenda Philips first gave me a copy of Howard Becker's book on writing in graduate school, and refused to let me get away with lazy writing. Lisa Henry made me recognize that my researcher soul is ethnographic. Lisa Zottarelli—your advice helped me gain my footing as a new academic, and for that I will always be grateful. Michelle Garcia and the rest of the amazing women at The OpEd Project gave me a different perspective on writing for a general audience and for making effective arguments (to be sure). Both the Creative Writing and Journalism programs at Texas Tech University started me on the path of professional writer.

Thanks also to Rosemary Condelario, Kris Clarke, Claire Sahlin, Dave Neal, Jessica Ringrose, Lisa Mazzei, Sandra Faulkner, Susan Harper, and Marni Binder for your suggestions of ethnographic inspiration.

Greg, Renn, and Rory—nothing happens without you. Thanks for understanding (and leaving me alone) when mama needed to work on her book. You are my love, my light, and my happiness.

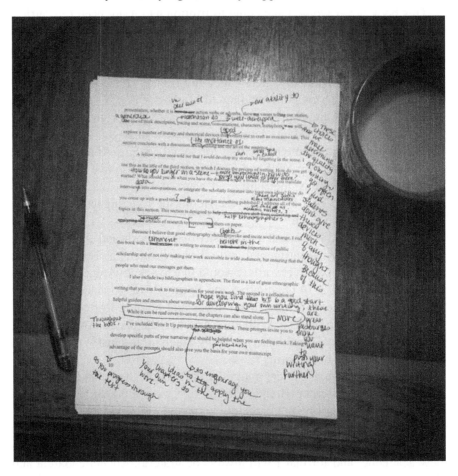

INTRODUCTION

Your field notes are compiled. Your interviews transcribed. You've written some memos and have hoarded all sorts of ephemera as data—maps, and drawings, and videos, and blogs, and technical reports, and websites, and photographs, and, and, and... You *know* your subject, you understand it, you've lived it. You're an ethnographer for goodness sakes! The only thing left for you to do is write it up.

You create a blank document on your computer. The cursor flashes on the screen.

Shit.

You freeze. Your mind as empty as the page.

The transition from field work to writing up our research can be rocky. Writing uses a different process, a different mindset, than what we've been doing in the field. Which is why I wrote this book. *Writing Ethnography* is intended for scholars in any discipline working with ethnographic methods, to help them to move from a sometimes seemingly insurmountable mound of data to a coherent written report, to help shift through the messiness and produce a written account of their work.

Anne Lamott's (1994) book, *Bird by Bird*, is one of my favorite writing memoirs. In introducing her own text, Lamott writes, "But you can't teach writing, people tell me. And I say, 'Who the hell are you, God's dean of admissions?'" Writing is a learned skill like any other. Perhaps writing comes easier for some people than for others, but we can all learn to write better.

Most ethnographers get a significant amount of training on the nuts and bolts of doing research in graduate school—if not in their classes, then in the process of doing their dissertations. Typically, ethnography students take courses on theory, methodology, data collection, and analysis. They learn about the underpinning philosophical stances that frame ethnographic practice and the ethical considerations associated with conducting qualitative research. They become well-versed on the practical aspects of how to conduct fieldwork, and how to collect data and keep field notes and memos. Many graduate programs, however, make an assumption that students already know how to write (surely you learned that in English 1013, if not in high school). Graduate programs are more likely to train students to be researchers, not to be writers.

This is not only a problem for graduate students. I've met many new faculty who have minimal experience writing for publication without the close assistance of a mentor, faculty who spend the first year or two on their tenure track floundering. Faculty who receive a letter from their tenure track committees during their third year that lament the fact that they haven't published enough and suggest they start looking for a new job.

You've worked too hard to let that happen.

Unless you land a job at a strictly teaching school, most universities expect their faculty to be published writers. Different schools have different expectations as to the volume of that writing, of course, or as to the prestige of the outlets you publish in, but nearly all universities expect that you will publish *something*. Newly minted PhDs on the job market should have evidence on their vitas that they will be successful on the tenure track (let's face it, a university's investment in you is huge, and they want you to make it). That evidence comes in the form of peer-reviewed publications. Likewise, faculty on the tenure track are expected to establish a solid research agenda and record of publications in their area of expertise.

Despite all this, however, ethnographers have a tendency to emphasize the 'ethno' of ethnography, and pay less attention to the 'graph'—to the writing of the ethnography.

And this is unfortunate.

Ultimately, to succeed in an academic career, a scholar must 'write up' their findings. As Westbrook (2008: 110–111) notes, "Writing is a professionally constitutive act, and one had better write something respectable. One's career, and so one's sense of self, are on the line, always." As academics, along with all the other roles we occupy, we are also expected to be professional writers. But that transition—from researching to writing—can be difficult, especially if we've had little training on how to make that transition.

The good news is that *Writing Ethnography* is here to help you.

"Nothing is stranger," Behar (1996: 5) writes, "than this business of humans observing other humans in order to write about them." I wrote this book to help you through that process, the process of writing up ethnography. This guide is for those of you who have been conducting ethnographic fieldwork, and are ready to begin publishing off your data. While directed to graduate students and new researchers, ethnographers in general might enjoy the ideas inside for honing their craft. Professional writer is part of the academic job description, perhaps one of the most important parts. I hope this book will help you in that role.

As a sociologist, many of my examples draw from the social sciences, and as an ethnographer myself, many of my examples come from my own experiences. However, as ethnographic practice has spread across the academy well outside of its anthropological and sociological roots, this book can be used across academic disciplines. *Writing Ethnography* can serve as either primary or secondary text in a variety of courses, including general and qualitative research methods, courses on ethnography and field work, and courses on academic writing and publishing across a diverse range of disciplines.

Many wonderful books have been written about the craft of ethnography and ethnographic practice. While I touch briefly on these topics, the focus of this book is on the final stages of that process, on the writing up of research. I've divided the subject matter in this book into brief chapters within four broad themes: Writing Ethnographically; Narrative Structures; Lingering in the Scene; and Writing to Connect and Writing for Social Change. While it can be read cover-to-cover, the chapters can also stand alone.

The first section, Writing Ethnographically, begins with brief history of ethnography (kept brief because I assume that readers of this book are already familiar with the practice of ethnography), followed by an overview of why researchers engage in this sort of work, and why it is important that we continue to do so. I follow that discussion with a transition into the idea of writing ethnography as creative nonfiction, a genre of its own but one that can inform and enhance our written products. Using creative nonfiction as our mode of operation, I explore the theories and foundations of what makes for a good story and how we can tap not only into the rational concrete aspects of our work, but also into the nonrational and emotive aspects of our ethnographies. Evocative, vulnerable writing draws our readers into our work, and makes our work resonate with readers long after they've finished reading, so I spend time discussing how to evoke vulnerability in your own writing.

As we write about real people who volunteered to participate in our research, I feel it is important for a text on writing ethnographies to include a discussion about the potential ethical issues specific to this type of writing itself. While most books on the practice of ethnography discuss ethical issues in the field, I briefly explore the ethics of representation. I follow this with a look at some of the major types of tales within the ethnographic tradition, and how they might inform your own writing. This leads into discussion of how to include researcher reflexivity in your written work as well as how consideration of audience shapes your final piece.

The second section of the book delves into issues of narrative structure. I review some techniques and particulars for writing good narratives. We start with an overview of narrative arcs and how those arcs play out in ethnographic writing. I talk about both the importance of and how to build tension in your work as a mean of pulling your reader through to the end of you story; about how to make your ethnography a page-turner your reader won't want to put down (and yes, such a unicorn of academic literature can exist). This is followed with a discussion of voice, and of how to find and develops yours. This section also begins to address issues of grammar and how the language we use shapes our presentation, whether it is in our use of action verbs or adverbs, in our ability to show the reader scenes from our field verses telling our stories, generous use of thick description, attention to pacing and scene, or well-developed conversations, characters, and metaphors. The stylistic choices we make determine the quality of our writing, yet often I find students don't give these literary devices much, if any, thought. Because of this we will explore a number of literary and rhetorical tools that good writers use to craft an evocative tale. This section concludes with a discussion about the importance of editing and about the art of the sentence.

A fellow writer once told me that I could develop my own stories by what she called 'lingering in the scene.' This is one of my favorite techniques for developing my own writing, and I use this as the title of the third section, in which I discuss the process of writing. How do you get started? How do you linger in a scene—and more important, how do you get your reader to linger in that scene with you? What should you do when you have the dreaded writer's block? How do you translate interview data into conversations, or integrate the scholarly literature into your own ideas? How do you come up with a good title, and how do you get something published? I address all of these topics in this section. This section is designed to help ethnographers represent the artifacts of their research on paper.

An ethic of social justice underlies all of my own academic work. Because I believe that good ethnography should both provoke and incite social change, I end this book with a comment on writing as a means to connect with others, to transcend the boundaries of our daily lives. I believe in the importance of public scholarship and of not only making our work accessible to wide audiences, but ensuring that the people who need our messages get them, and I address some suggestions for how to do this in this section.

I also include two bibliographies in appendices. The first is a list of great ethnographic writing that you can look to for inspiration for your own work. The second is a collection of helpful guides and memoirs about writing. While I hope that you find *Writing Ethnography* is a good start for developing your own writing, the references in the appendices are great resources for pushing your writing further.

Throughout the text, I've included Write It Up prompts to encourage you to apply the techniques in the chapters to your own writing. These prompts invite you to develop specific parts of your narrative and should be helpful when you are feeling stuck. Taking advantage of the prompts as you progress through the text should also give you a strong foundation for your own manuscript. Instructors may wish to use the prompts either as take-home or in-class writing assignments.

One of my own academic interests is the process of conducting intellectual work. I enjoy reading about other writers' processes—what works, what doesn't, where to find inspiration, and what to do to keep the creativity flowing. I discuss many of these ideas throughout this book. But none of this is prescriptive. While writers use a lot of the same techniques, our approaches to the creative process may differ. That's kind of a definition of creativity, right? Making it your own. What works for me may not work for you, and the opposite might be true. I encourage you to try out a variety of these ideas to help figure out what works well for you and to incorporate them into your own writing. Doing so will enhance not only your own creative process but also to enhance your final products.

We have our goal: Write compelling stories.

Let's get started.

SECTION I

WRITING ETHNOGRAPHICALLY

A BRIEF HISTORY OF ETHNOGRAPHY

Once largely the purview of anthropologists and sociologists, researchers in other disciplines have taken up ethnographic methods to delve into a variety of social groups and situations. Nurse ethnographers research topics such as the work of nurse practitioners in acute-care settings (Williamson et al., 2012), or nursing education (Malinsky et al., 2010), or nurses as agents of healing and social change in the midst of political revolution (Pine, 2013). Ethnographers in education write about research ethics (Dennis, 2010), or teacher education (Frank, 2004), or health education among traditional healers (Simmons, 2011). Dance ethnographers explore specific dance cultures (Paulson, 2011) or even lap dancing (Colosi, 2010). And so on across the academy.

Keeping an overview of ethnography brief is difficult due to the wonderful diversity in approaches to ethnographic practice. Any generalized statements about the field are understandably contestable, so I invite you to read further if you would like to gain a greater understanding of the richness of this line of inquiry. I encourage broad reading of both completed ethnographies and writings on ethnographic methods. Read general books on writing as well. Get a feel for writing styles, identify both what writers do well in their written accounts and what is problematic. To help you get started, I've included bibliographies in Appendix I and II.

Ethnography is a tool, a method for researchers in just about any academic discipline who want to understand a particular slice of social life. Ethnographers are culture detectives. We immerse ourselves in a field—a setting in which social interactions occur—living for a certain time and to the extent possible, in a specific social reality under study. We then share the experience of that social reality with others through our writing. Our fieldwork can occur anywhere, in all sorts of settings, such as hospitals or in jails, or among gangs or cult members, or with dance troupes or artist colonies, or even online in chat groups or massive multiplayer online video games. Ethnographers identify a group of people or an activity of interest to them, try to understand what happens in that setting through our fieldwork, and then explain it to outsiders with our written accounts. Today's ethnographies are often multi-sited and multi-media, taking place in both physical and virtual spaces.

Traditionally, ethnographers focused their efforts on understanding a particular culture. Historically this was nearly always a culture different from that of the researcher. I would be remiss not to acknowledge that early ethnographic accounts were particularly interested in researching in 'exotic' locales. These projects were often associated with imperialist tendencies and the othering of humans (oftentimes to the level of dehumanization). That history has been difficult to transcend—even today, there are ethnographers operating in war conditions with the explicit goal of military advantage (Kusiak, 2008). We need to both problematize and be cognizant of the moral and ethical implications of our work, and ensure that we don't replicate that othering today. Much has been written on this topic, and I encourage you to read up on it.

We can find the roots of ethnographic practice in the disciplines of anthropology and sociology, early in the establishment of these fields as academic disciplines. While there is significant overlap between the anthropological and sociological traditions (Van Maanen, 2011), I will briefly outline the history of ethnography below. This is a general overview and not meant to be a comprehensive account of this history; indeed there has been more than a century of work on this topic, and students interested in this history should research it further.

We'll begin with anthropology. The earliest anthropological research was marked with excursions to exotic locales as a rite of passage (Van Maanen, 2011). Budding anthropologists would load up their gear and travel to some remote location, to hopefully find an as yet undiscovered tribe of indigenous peoples hidden away in the jungle and attempt to understand their 'primitive' ways. Perhaps rightly criticized for their imperialistic orientations, anthropologists of the 1800s sought primarily to understand very 'othered' cultures. Through the 'savage' case, they believed they could better understand the process of 'civilization' (Van Maanen, 2011). To bolster the legitimacy of this work, and to differentiate the discipline from travel writing, they drew heavily on positivistic modes of inquiry, and techniques of categorization and classification of humans.

Enter Bronislaw Malinowski. Malinowski is generally credited with the development of in-depth, scientific field research. His 1922 work, *Argonauts of the Western Pacific*, gained acclaim as one of the foundational texts of ethnography, and "by the late 1920s fieldwork and the image of the scientifically trained fieldworker stalking the wiley native in his natural habitat had become the cornerstone of anthropology" (Van Maanen, 2011: 17). For decades after Malinowski, early career anthropologists were expected to travel to a different, often remote, location and prove their worth through field work (and in some departments that is still the norm).

Sociologists were not immune to the othering of peoples, although their field was different. Rather than travel to a different location to decipher radically different cultures, sociologists looked to deviant subcultures in their own neighborhoods. Sociological ethnography was based largely on social reform movements of the early 1900s. In the United States, the major impetus for sociological ethnography came from the Chicago School in the area of urban ethnography. Park, Thomas, Burgess, and their students "explored the city as if it were a remote and exotic setting" (Van Maanen, 2011). Their writings often had a documentary, journalistic style (Park having been trained as a journalist). Sociologists sought to uncover 'social facts' in the Durkheimian tradition, and present them in written form with little commentary and analysis. These researchers explored the margins of society on either side of the social class structure (although more often the lower economic end), considering both the impoverished and the power elite, once again othering a group of people. As Westbook (2008: 88) notes, "with the dearth of truly exotic subjects, there has been a notable tendency to exoticize the unfortunate."

As both disciplines evolved, ethnography as method gained supremacy among anthropologists. Sociologists in turn embraced quantitative positivism as their method of choice, and while some still practiced ethnography, its status in sociology did not fare as well.

The disciplinary divisions between anthropology and sociology have blurred and eroded in recent decades. Historically, anthropologists were primarily inclined to study non-Western cultures while their counterparts in sociology studied Western cultures. This distinction delineated the disciplinary boundaries. Today those boundaries are much less rigid, and anthropologists can be found conducting fieldwork in Western urban areas, while sociologists may be found traipsing through lesser economically developed areas of the globe.

In addition, after troubling their imperialistic roots, both disciplines have amassed significant bodies of writing on the ethics of ethnography and have sought to minimize any violence on their research participants (even reframing the involvement of the people in their studies, from thinking of people as research subjects to working with them as full participants in their projects). They've also embraced indigenous scholarship and sought to devise methods to work in collaboration with the peoples they are researching. Today's ethnographers attempt to dismantle hierarchical relationships between researcher and researched, and to be on constant alert for issues of participant exploitation and violence. This often involves co-constructed narratives, member checking, action research, and other built-in assurances that the relationship is beneficial to both researcher and participant.

Meanwhile, ethnographic practice has expanded throughout the social sciences and much of the humanities. Researchers from across the academy interested in understanding a group of people or type of social interaction in depth have become ethnographers.

There has also been a turn inwards where ethnographers look to their own cultures. Researching 'at home' has become common practice, with researchers delving into their local communities and groups they are part of (Gullion, 2015). Autoethnographers turn a critical lens on themselves, using their own experiences as data (after all, what other data would you know better?).

Write It Up

1. How does your specific discipline shape your research? In what ways do you transcend disciplinary boundaries?
2. Describe your field setting. Why was this the appropriate setting for your subject?
3. What safeguards do you take in your own research to ensure that the people you work with are participants rather than subjects? How do you ensure that they are not only treated ethically, but in a socially just manner?

CHAPTER 2

WHY ETHNOGRAPHY?

Van Maanen (2011: 2) writes that "fieldwork is one answer—some say the best—to the question of how the understanding of others, close or distant, is achieved." Ethnographers immerse themselves in a culture (typically) not of their own, to achieve an in-depth understanding of that culture. As ethnographies are usually conducted over a long period of time (often years), ethnographers participate in the unfolding of a scene, and share in the community experience. Projects range from studies of the mundane—such as an ethnographic study on table arrangements and background noise at a café (Whyte & Buckner, 2001)—to the specialized—like one of women's artistic gymnastics (Barker-Ruchti & Tinning, 2010)—to the virtual—such as an ethnography of the massive multiplayer online video game, World of Warcraft (Nardi, 2010). Ethnographies ultimately have in common the attempt of a researcher to understand what it is like *to be* part of this group and to then express and often translate that experience for people who are not part of that group. This type of research is both a highly engaged and interpretive process.

The field is the physical (or virtual) space in which our research takes place. Fieldwork allows us to gain a depth of understanding of our research topic that cannot be captured in snapshot research methods (such as surveys or one-time interviews). Today, a particular respondent might score low on an anxiety scale. Next week, she might score high on the same scale. What has changed? Snapshot research methods cannot answer that question, but ethnography can. Lived experience is dynamic, and one of the best ways to capture that movement is through engaged ethnographic practice. The ethnographer witnesses, uncovers, and documents the motion and fluidity of life.

Thus, it is important for us as writers to portray that fluidity in our written accounts of our fieldwork. In writing ethnography we (re)present those dynamics for our readers. We tell our readers the story of what happened. Ethnographic writing (and reading for that matter) is different from that of quantitative approaches to research. Richardson (2009) writes: "Unlike quantitative work which can carry its meaning in its tables and summaries, qualitative work carries its meanings in its entire text. Just as a piece of literature is not equivalent to its 'plot summary,' qualitative research is not contained in its abstract. Qualitative research has to be read, not scanned; its meaning is in the reading." Our job as writers of ethnography is to express that meaning to our readers through our texts. To illuminate the drama of events, to embrace and express the emotion, rather than distance ourselves from the researched through percentages, tables, and graphs.

Ethnographers are the witnesses. We listen to and retell stories—like oral historians before us, we are the keepers of the stories. We keep them alive. We honor the people and places and things in our ethnographies. And herein lies our need to write well. "The act of writing," Madden (2010: 153) writes, "is more than simply reporting on the interpretations that spring from the primary and secondary ethnographic data. The act of ethnographic writing is a form of collating, reporting, and interpreting at the same time; it is both systematic and artful."

Writing—(re)presenting culture on the page—is just as important as data collection techniques. And ethnography is not only embodied storytelling—we also theorize through our narrative forms. Like writers of creative nonfiction, we tell compelling stories with our ethnographic data. Indeed, "the more theoretically relevant a piece of ethnographic work is, the more

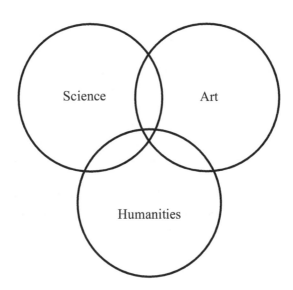

Figure 1. Intersecting domains

it is able to travel from local community concerns and substantive area to capture wider academic interest and make a more lasting contribution to scholarship," Puddephatt and colleagues (2009: 2) remind us. As we are academics and not journalists, we also embed our work in larger academic conversations. We interpret and analyze events through our disciplinary lens.

Ethnography occupies an interesting interrogative space at the intersection of the sciences, humanities, and the arts. Because of the lived reality of the groups and activities we research, and their dynamic nature, good ethnographers utilize all three domains in their research. We can (and good ethnographers do) also use tools from all three domains. Sometimes the answers we seek aren't where we look. Embracing interdisciplinarity and even transcending disciplinary boundaries leads to both a richer ethnography and also to a richer understanding of our research subject.

Flyvbjerg (2001:18) writes, "Where science does not reach, art, literature, and narrative often help us comprehend the reality in which we live." He continues, "Nietzsche suggests that the central task for human beings is not the Socratic one of making knowledge cerebral and rational but instead one of making it bodily and intuitive." Luckily for us, as academic nomads, we have the tools at our disposal to strive for both.

Write It Up

1. Explain to your reader why you chose an ethnographic approach to your study and why this approach is the best one for answering your particular research questions.
2. Discuss your method and data collection. How did you enter/exit the field? How did you build relationships with the people in your project? What data did you collect? How did you manage and analyze your data? Explain your process to your reader.

CREATIVE NONFICTION IN ETHNOGRAPHY

Just as we straddle disciplinary conventions, ethnographers also straddle writing boundaries. Our writing tends to seek a balance, or perhaps a blurring, of academic and lay worlds, and has the potential to reach a large audience. "Ethnographers occupy a literary borderland," Van Maanen (2011: xiii), writes, "somewhere between writers who research for very general audiences and those who reach for a specialized few." One way to do this is to embrace the techniques of creative nonfiction in our own writing.

After I suggested this one evening in a research methods class, one of the graduate students told me that she had never written creatively, and that she didn't think she can write anything other than an 'academic' article in an (admittedly boring) dispassionate voice. I should add that this student was also one of the funniest people I've ever met, and had me practically rolling on the floor laughing at every class session. "But you tell wonderful stories all the time," I said. "Write in that voice. Write in your story-telling voice."

While some are more interesting than others, we are all storytellers. Yes, it's not how we are trained to write when we write academic work, but aside from that, we convey information to other humans daily through storytelling. "Stories are the most fundamental and profound way we have of engaging with our fellow human beings," DasGupta writes (2014: 6). When your friend asks how your day went and you describe a colleague who went ballistic and yelled at the department chair in a faculty meeting, you are telling a story. When you call your mom and tell her about your doctor's visit, or when you explain the definition of a key term to your students using an example from your own experience, you are telling a story.

Jack Hart (2011: 5) writes, "Storytelling has such wide application because, at its root, it serves universal human needs. Story makes sense out of a confusing universe by showing us how one action leads to another. It teaches us how to live by discovering how our fellow human beings overcome the challenges in their lives. And it helps us discover the universals that bind us to everything around us."

While we may not be used to writing this way as part of our academic work, the practice of storytelling is not as foreign as many academics might at first glance believe. This is particularly the case for ethnographers. Most of our fieldwork is spent collecting stories; through writing up what happened there, we honor those stories. When we write creatively, we are simply telling the story of what happened in the field. And let's face it, as Madden (2010: 6) writes: "An ethnography is ultimately a story that is backed up by reliable ethnographic data and the authority that comes from active ethnographic engagement."

Creative writing captures our storytelling voice on paper. Unfortunately, many of us are resistant to using creative writing in our academic work. When academics embrace creative writing styles, we may be asked by our colleagues if our work is science or literature, and expected to classify our work in one realm or the other (and if you are working in a social sciences department, the science category is almost always more highly respected than the literature category). But I believe that this distinction, between technical scientific writing and creative literary forms is, and rightly should be, transgressed in ethnographic writing. Today's ethnographies range from positivist research reports to outright fictional accounts based in research (Gullion, 2014; Leavy, 2015), and do so for good reason. If you need to push back against criticisms against writing creatively, remember that ethnographers use scientific methods—methods that are systematic—and we then represent our findings with a variety of literary (and/or artistic) devices. Our writing up is called a representation, but should more rightly be viewed as a (re)presentation, we are (re)presenting what happened in the field. And we have a multitude of forms at our disposal to do that (re)presenting in a manner that is the most authentic to our findings and to our participants.

I personally find writing that blends poetic moments with academic ones most appealing. More than border crossings, they are border disruptions, lines of flight into different ways of understanding the subject. The evaluation criteria for this type of work is less about whether or not our work comes across sounding 'scientific' and more about whether or not our work illuminates understanding of the subject under study. Do we create new knowledge or new ways of knowing a thing? Does our voice penetrate and contribute to the ongoing conversation about a particular subject? Does our work provoke others to think about our subject differently? Did we act in an ethical, transparent manner, and were we clear about this in our writing? If so, I think we've done our due diligence.

Criticisms of ethnographic writing—particularly of more experimental forms—such as, 'is this scholarly?' or worse, 'is this research?' are tired misunderstandings of qualitative inquiry (or perhaps obstinate inabilities to attempt to understand *decades* of scholarship that addresses these questions).

Nonetheless, there is a possibility that these questions will be lobbed at you when you present your work to colleagues less familiar with this type of work, and you should be prepared to answer them. Try this: While we use literary and artistic devices to represent our work, it is scholarly, in that we "place the real life story within a larger social, political, or institutional issue or research question" (Goodall, 2008: 34). Teasing out the embeddedness of the story within a larger milieu, with all the accompanying implications: this is what scholars *do*. This type of work is research in that we utilize a variety of accepted methodologies to know the world. We find stories within stories, events in intersections, and the telling of these stories adds to the ongoing scholarly conversation (and sometimes sparks new ones).

And then you can blow a big raspberry at them behind their backs.

Write It Up

1. Do you have any hesitations to writing creatively? What are they? Write them out and then write an argument against each.
2. List three criticisms that colleagues might have of your work. Write rebuttals for each.

CHAPTER 4

WHAT MAKES A STORY GREAT?

Now that we've (more or less) embraced the idea that we can write ethnography using creative nonfiction, let's look at what makes for a good story.

A down-on-his-luck high school chemistry teacher has a really bad day. While at his second job (washing his students' cars at a local car wash), he collapses, is rushed to the hospital in an ambulance, and is diagnosed with lung cancer. His insurance is terrible, and oh, yeah, he also has a pregnant wife and a disabled son at home. In a fortuitous turn of events, the chemistry teacher discovers a quick way to make gobs of money, one that he is particularly well-suited for: He's going to cook meth, and use a former student to sell it.

In the hit TV show *Breaking Bad*, viewers watch that chemistry teacher— Walter White—descend into a violent drug subculture. The story pulls viewers along in sympathy with a man who becomes a drug lord, all the while remaining a sympathetic character. We *like* Walter White (most of the time). His actions make sense to us, given the circumstances he finds himself in.

Breaking Bad is a great story. But why? What makes a story great?

If we boil down narrative theory, we can distill the essence of good storytelling. A good story has relatable characters, who want something, and overcome obstacles in its pursuit (Hart, 2011). Walter White is a relatable character. He's Everyman. He's a middle class guy with a mediocre life that seems to be steadily going downhill. He works two jobs, both of which are demeaning and do nothing to fulfill his human potential. He wants something—desperately. He wants to make sure that his family is taken care of. He's worried the lung cancer will kill him, and he will leave his wife and children destitute. He can't have that, because at heart his overwhelming drive is to protect them. And boy does he ever have to overcome obstacles in pursuit of the money he needs for his treatment and for his family. The world he steps into is violent, cold, calculating, and unforgiving, and he has to participate in it fully to survive. Throughout the TV series, we accompany Walter on a journey of exquisite transformation, from Everyman to Drug

Kingpin. And all along the way, it makes sense to us. We *get* Walter. We understand how that transformation takes place.

A great story evokes images, sounds, sensations, feelings, emotions, memories—all of these qualities in the reader's mind. But this is not as daunting as it sounds. Remember that all readers come to your work with their own reference points, their own imaginations and prior experiences. A few words can evoke a character, place, or feeling in their minds.

Let's try an example. My friend Karen was in a car wreck when she was a teenager. The driver, her best friend, drunk out of her mind, crashed the car into a tree. Karen didn't have on a seatbelt. She was ejected face-first through the windshield, narrowly missing the tree. After dozens of surgeries, Karen still has subtle scars on the left hand side of her face, and she complains that she can't do anything with her hair because of the roadmap of scars on her scalp.

Could your picture Karen and the wreck in your mind? There are lots of details I didn't give you. I didn't tell you what kind of car the friend drove, or what color it was. I didn't tell you how big the tree was, or how fast the car was going, or even, really how long ago this happened (how old is Karen now?). I didn't say much about what Karen looks like—is her hair dark or light, straight or curly? Does it stick up straight or in globs? Nonetheless, as you were reading, you probably formed a pretty good picture in your head of what happened to her. The scene evoked images, feelings, sensations (did you imagine how that face-first ejection through the windshield felt?), perhaps even sounds in your mind. This is what I mean by evocative writing. We connect with the reference points already in our readers' minds. Our reader knows what a car is and what a car smashing into a tree looks like. Our reader probably has a good sense of (or could imagine) what would happen to someone in that situation who wasn't wearing a seatbelt. Our reader understands about scars and surgeries and hairlines. We connect to those reference points with our own story, make it real for them, in our writing.

Good stories also draw on our emotions. There is some sort of vulnerability to them. We can connect to what is happening in the story on a visceral level. As writers, we have the power to evoke all sorts of emotions in our readers. Horror stories evoke fear, perhaps disgust, and also feelings of strength (defeating the enemy). Love stories evoke affection of course, but also loneliness, longing, happiness, and contentment. An ethnography of a natural disaster might bring up feelings of loss, frustration, and distress. An ethnography of an animal laboratory might bring up feelings of compassion, tedium, and the excitement of a new discovery. Like the evocation of sensory details, writing vulnerably connects our writing to our reader's emotional reference points.

Finally, good stories follow some sort of logical narrative arc, a storyline or plot line. The events in a good story are ordered and parceled out in a way that keeps the reader wanting to know more. That's what we mean when we say a book is a page-turner—the reader doesn't want to put the book down because they need to know what happens next.

In telling your own story, your own ethnography, what do you want the reader to know? What do you want the reader to imagine, to feel? What do you want the reader to take away from the experience of reading your words? Most academic writing takes the form of reports. In my discipline of sociology, a typical research article has set subject headings: Introduction, Literature Review, Methods, Findings, Discussion, and Conclusion. Researchers share a lot of great information in this format, and I don't want to detract from that. But this form is probably not the best way to share an ethnography because so much of what makes an ethnography wonderful is lost when you try to cobble it together into a report. "Stories convey experience," Hart (2011: 57) writes, "but reports convey information, often great gobs of it....We need gobs of information to operate in the modern world, and most of the time we don't want to work our way through narrative to get to the main point. But stories offer rewards beyond raw information, the kind that yield meaning by recreating life as it's lived. Stories emphasize process, rather than outcomes." This is the goal of ethnography, isn't it? To "yield meaning by recreating life as it's lived." To "emphasize process, rather than outcomes."

Let's look more at the nuts and bolts of how to make that happen.

Write It Up

1. Identify a story that you find compelling. It can be written or visual. What details and emotions are evoked in your own imagination?
2. What narratives do you find compelling? Examine their underlying structure. What does the author or creator do to hold your interest?

EVOCATIVE STORYTELLING

As I mentioned above, we want our stories to be evocative, to bring forth sensory details in our readers' imaginations. Evocative stories capture and hold our readers' interest and keep them thinking about our story long after they've finished reading. We want people to ruminate over our words. Let's look at evocative storytelling in more detail with some specific techniques that you can use in your own writing.

Goodall (2008: 27) writes that evocative storytelling has several characteristics. First of all, an evocative story includes some sort of conflict, some central problem that needs to be overcome. Think about your own field work. Somewhere along the way, if you did your due diligence as a researcher, something, some problem or conflict, presented itself in your group during your fieldwork. That problem could be grand or small, but a problem happened, and someone in your project needed to solve that problem.

Much of my ethnography, *Fracking the Neighborhood,* deals with the conflicts that arose between residents who live above one of the richest natural gas fields in the world, and the natural gas industry who wanted to drill under their homes for that gas. I also explored the failures of governmental regulatory agencies to intervene in those conflicts. The residents were the underdog of the story, and throughout the tale, they were repeatedly knocked down, as in this example:

> Joyce's home sits in the middle of three natural gas sites. One of the pads is 200 feet from her house. The others are within five hundred feet. I can see two of them from windows in her kitchen. The third takes up most of the view out of her living room windows.
>
> "They came onto our neighbor's property in August 2009, on a Saturday. I was in the living room, working out on my elliptical. Through the window I saw trucks starting to show up, and I thought, that's odd. But they let people come over and fish out of their ponds, so it's not super odd. But they were more than what looked normal. And a few minutes later, my neighbor called me and he said, 'they're coming to put in a well, and there's nothing that I can do about it.' And she told me, the

wife told me, later, that the way that she found out that they're going to do that was: previously, there was a white pickup truck out there on their property, and she thought it was odd. So she went out to talk to them and she said, 'Do you want to fish?' Because lots of people come out and they want fish. I guess that's normal out here. They'll drive by and they'll see somebody's pond and they will go up and ask, 'Can we fish?' It's kind of the neighborly sort of thing. He was very apologetic, but he said, 'I'm sorry ma'am but I'm actually looking to see where I'm going to put my bulldozer.' And she said, 'What bulldozer?' And he said, 'I'm sorry, we're… they're getting ready to put in a well here.' So, it was a subcontractor that told her."

"It's on her property? Someone just shows up to her property and says we're going to drill?" I ask.

Joyce nods. "It's like we're not even here."

David and Goliath stories work for good reason. Readers enjoy the struggle and victory of an underdog. And if David didn't win, that's okay too. Leave the reader upset about the outcome—that may be motivation for them to take action.

Evocative stories include conflict, something that stands in the path of your characters' desires. Goodall also notes that the reader should be able to personally connect on some level with the story. They should form some sort of visceral connection that makes them care about what happens to the people in your story. Many readers of *Fracking the Neighborhood* probably do not live in an area with natural gas development. They don't personally cope with the nuisance and health threats that come with living near this sort of industrial activity. So why should they care about what I have to say? To help them connect to my story, I looked for ways in which they types of events in the narrative could be familiar (and important) to them. While the specific incidents may differ, if I could find points of connection I not only could attract readers, but I could also bring empathy to the story as a whole. In *Fracking the Neighborhood*, many of the parents I spoke with talked about their fears of how the pollution from the natural gas wells might damage their children's health. Many parents can relate to that fear, and understand the desire to protect their children, no matter the circumstance. The home owners in the story discussed issues of property rights, and how even though they own the property, a company is legally allowed to come on their land and drill for natural gas, and they cannot refuse it. Other homeowners can probably understand why the people in my story are upset. Most homeowners can probably imagine how distraught they would be if some company tore up their backyard with a bunch of heavy equipment spewing exhaust into the air and they were not legally allowed to stop them. People in the story express their frustration with the government, and discuss how difficult their interactions with government bureaucracy are. Many Americans have felt similar frustrations. These points of connection help make the story relatable. While the readers may not live with natural gas development, they can, drawing on their own experiences, imagine what that might be like for people who do live with it. We want to identify possible points of connection between the reader and the narrative and make those points explicit.

Goodall's third point is that an evocative story should foster continuing curiosity—that is, if the reader sticks with the story, if the reader reads the story to the end, there will be a payoff. Some truth will be revealed. Perhaps the conflict will resolve. Perhaps the characters will transform in meaningful ways. This is interrelated with Goodall's last point, which is that an evocative story has some sort of climactic satisfaction. The reader should feel that their journey—the journey of having read your writing—was worth their time. That they got something out of their time investment. Maybe they learned something new, or felt something unexpected, or experienced an emotional release, or just had a good time reading your work. Hart (2011: 17) writes that "a compelling story must immerse readers in another world, carrying them away from their mundane daily cares." It is probably safe to say that most ethnographers find their own research fascinating—otherwise why spend so much time and energy in the field? Convey that fascination to your reader—immerse them in the alternate reality that is your fieldwork with your words. Ethnographies have the potential to transport readers to all sorts of alternative worlds. Use this to your advantage and take your reader to new places:

High school gyms all have the same smell, that teenaged hormone infused dirty sweat smell. Grant surveyed the space. Painted paper banners decorated either end of the large room with school spirit. "Go Mavs!" they read. He thought that was a stupid mascot, the Mavericks. It was a horse, which he didn't really get. Better to have something fierce, like a lion or a bear. Or his personal favorite, the Round Rock Dragons. Now that was a cool name for a mascot.

A horse raised on its hind legs, steam marks indicated at its snout, pawed at the scoreboard, painted in blue. Today the gym was silent. He enjoyed how the spongy floor flexed beneath his boots. Bits of blue and white plastic pompom fodder fray hid under the wooden bleachers, pulled out from the last pep rally. Everyone was really pissed off when they closed the schools. No school, no football. And folks around here lived for football. Despite their dumb mascot, Grant loved to go to the games. Madison had a great coach, and they went to state almost every year. Unlike the university team, which blew.

"Can you show me the climate controls?" he asked the principal. His words echoed in the vast emptiness of the space. "How cold can you get it in here?"

"I'll show you, over here. I'm not sure. We've never had a need for that. Before." The principal opened the machine closet at the far corner of the room.

The colder the room, the longer the bodies would keep. There would still be decomposition, they couldn't bring the temp down enough to freeze them, but they could drop it pretty far. When he was in Kosovo with the UN, Grant encountered tons of bodies that had been left out in the sun. The stench was indescribable. He didn't want a repeat of that.

The State Emergency Ops Centre had a guy on his way to help them rig the system to keep the temp really low. This fascinated Grant. How does one get that job, school gym/morgue converter? Did this require specialized training, or was it a self-taught skill? Probably pays well. How many could there be? Getting the body bags turned out to be easy. The state had thousands of them stockpiled after the Amerithrax attacks, for bioterrorism.

"Do you think we will have trouble getting people to come to the basketball games after this?" the principal asked, only half joking. Grant felt bad for him. Four high schools in the district and his gym gets picked to be the city's temporary morgue. It has to do with security. Madison was on the edge of town, easier to secure.

"Sure. Coach Jameson knows what he's doing. I'd expect the girls will take us to state again this year. No one will want to miss that. Of course your floor will have to be replaced. I'm afraid it will be ruined," Grant said.

"It's a nice floor," the principal said. "Cost a fortune."

"I think they'll come to the games," Grant said. (Gullion 2014: 97–98)

We want to write stories that will stick with our readers long after they finished reading our writing. To take them to new places. To evoke their imaginations and their emotional vulnerability. To make the journey worthwhile.

Write It Up

1. As academics, we are always reading. Make a list of evocative stories (fiction and nonfiction) that stuck with you long after you finished reading them. What made them evocative? Tease out the techniques the authors used and apply them to your own work.
2. Identify the payoff of your work. What do you hope will resonate with your readers long after they've finished reading your work?

CHAPTER 6

VULNERABILITY IN WRITING

I've written about evoking emotions and emotional vulnerability in our readers. Now we're going to concentrate on your own vulnerability as a writer.

To get the sort of deep emotional terrain that moves your reader into your story, you have to be open to emotional vulnerability yourself. You have to be what Behar (1996) calls a vulnerable observer. We as writers have to feel that emotion to get it on the page. We have to make ourselves vulnerable, and that can be tough for a lot of us, especially if we have been indoctrinated with the notion that science should be dispassionate, and void of affect.

One of the best places to get a feel for this sort of writing is to look to autoethnography. Autoethnographers critically situate their own experience to inform larger intellectual questions. Sophie Tamas (2011: 70–71) does a beautiful job integrating her own anxieties about the research process in this passage from her book, *Life After Leaving: The Remains of Spousal Abuse*. Incorporating a variety of representational techniques, here her text is written as a play, as discussion between herself and her dog Cricket about how her research is progressing:

Sophie: It's terrible. I'm totally incompetent.

Cricket: Not entirely. You can use the hunches, tensions, and disjunctions in your own life. Let it go from clarity to fuzziness. Your questions can change as you go along, and you might not see what was answered until you get to the end of it.

Sophie: Please don't tell me to trust the process.

Cricket: (laughing) Okay. Don't trust the process. See how that goes.

Sophie: (shaking her head) My dog is a mindfulness meditation guru.

Throughout her work, Tamas finds herself dealing with tensions between studying a research population as both a researcher and a member of that group, and of practicing feminist research ethics, all the while searching for her own place in that process. As a researcher who has grappled with similar questions, I find myself identifying with her predicaments.

Drawing on your own emotional reserves while you write helps create additional spaces for connection between you and your readers. I am not a member of Tamas' study group, and her project, while both interesting and informative, is outside of my scholarly area of interest. But I feel connected to her as a researcher because she allows herself to be vulnerable, to express her own feelings about research.

I recently presented a series of poems at a conference (Gullion, 2014). I crafted them from interview transcripts. When I finished reading, the room was silent.

"Um, okay, that's it. Thank you," I said, and awkwardly sat back down. The next presenter got up to speak. I fought feelings of nausea and tried to listen to her, with a nagging at the back of my mind: Did they *get* it? Did they *like* it? And the biggie: *Am I a fraud?*

After the conference session ended a small woman from the audience approached me. "Very powerful," she said in a heavy Scandinavian accent. Others around her nodded.

That was the extent of feedback from the audience, but I felt good about it. Sometimes, particularly when a piece *is* very powerful, people need time to process their emotional responses.

I've often received feedback that something I've written is "very powerful." I believe the act of vulnerable observing (Behar, 1996) is what garners that response. Allowing ourselves to be emotionally vulnerable as we write opens the flow of feeling onto the page. We invite readers to experience a depth of responses while engaging with the scene.

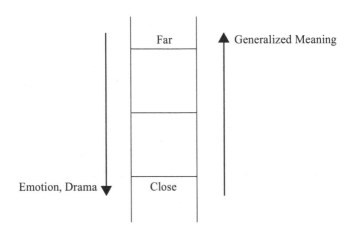

Figure 2. The ladder of abstraction
Source: Hart (2011)

To write vulnerably, we can consider the emotional distance between the reader and our subject in our writing. Hart (2011: 55) recommends we think of that distance as a ladder, as what he refers to as the 'ladder of abstraction.' The lower down on the ladder, the closer the distance to the subject, and the greater the evocation of emotion. We can move up and down the ladder in the course of our piece.

When we close distance in a scene, we provide first-hand details and drama. This is what evokes emotion in our reader. As we pull back from a particular scene, the details become vaguer, more generalized, but this is where we convey overall meaning for our reader.

Let's take a look at an example. I conducted research on people with cancer who believe that their cancer was caused by something in their natural environment (Gullion, 2015a). In this paragraph, I move up the ladder of abstraction, using distance to discuss meaning in the data:

When confronted with a cancer diagnosis, many people seek to learn the cause. Knowing the cause may serve to externalize responsibility— "it was not my fault that I got cancer." This knowing also serves to quell the fears of the well—"if I know the cause of someone else's cancer, I can avoid that cause and protect myself."

Cancer can be an emotional subject, but the above paragraph is distanced from the visceral reactions that cancer patients can express. We get information about meaning—about the roles of responsibility and fear, so the stage has been set for emotional engagement, but as this is not yet personal, we maintain some distance.

Now let's move down the ladder of abstraction, to the space of vulnerability and emotion, with a closeness to the subject. I represented the interview data using a 'found poetry' method. In the project, I explored the ways in which some cancer patients attribute factors in their environment (such as chemical pollution or radiation) as having caused their cancer (Gullion, 2015a). I pulled statements from interview transcripts to represent each theme I found in the research. I'd hoped for a visceral response on the part of the reader, a powerful way for the reader to connect to the cancer patients who participated in the study. I did not simply want to state that some patients believe (and are upset) that a toxin in their physical environment caused their cancer. While that is true, I wanted the reader to *feel* it, to connect with the patients on a emotional level. To move down the ladder of abstraction, we are closer to the patients themselves. See if you can feel the difference between the paragraph example about and the poems below.

Dick Cheney Gave Me Cancer

Dick Cheney gave me cancer.
I bought him a new heart,
My tax dollars went to giving him a heart.
His Halliburton, gas drilling, radiation release, exposure—
Now I have cancer.

I don't feel it's a fair trade.
He's rich and I'm going broke
Trying to pay for cancer treatments.
I'm collateral damage.
I'm a statistic trying to be the voice
Of statistics that don't have a voice because
They lost their battle and I haven't
Lost mine.
Yet.
I know this cancer will kill me.
But not yet.

Gullion (2015a)

This is the final poem in the series:

Last Word

My cancer robbed me of a normal
Life. I can't have kids. I can't work.
I'm mad that people go through this
Who don't have to. Because environmental
Stuff can be controlled.
Should be controlled.

It pisses me off. I'm gonna start
Crying in a second.

[Tape recorder turned off].

Write It Up

1. Write about your own feelings about your ethnographic research. Write several scenes from your project in which your own emotions were brought to the surface. For example, did you ever cry (or try hard not to) during an interview?
2. Choose one instance from your research. Write about from both a far and close perspective.

CHAPTER 7

ETHICAL ISSUES IN ETHNOGRAPHIC WRITING

Now that we have a sense of what makes for a good story and some ways in which we can connect with our readers, let's turn our attention to the ethics of writing ethnography. Ethnographers grapple with a number of ethical decisions throughout the research process, and ethical questions continue to present themselves even in our writing up. In writing our results, we have two major issues we must address: protection of participant privacy, and transparency to our readers. And unfortunately for us as writers, these two issues can come into conflict with each other.

We must, of course, adhere to all of our participant protections as outlined and approved by our Institutional Review Boards. The details of those protections may vary by institution, but generally speaking people who participate in our research projects are afforded a strict right to privacy. This is one important area in which ethnographic research differs from journalism—we usually do not name our sources in order to protect them from any possible harm.

On the other hand, we have a duty to our readers. We want our readers to trust what we write. We don't want to deceive them in the process of protecting the privacy of our participants. If we decide to use a composite character, or if we are otherwise altering details, we must be honest about what we did, how we did it, and why. We don't want to misrepresent what happened or what we found—we need to maintain a delicate balance between openness with the research process and protection of the people in the project.

Duneier (2011: 2) argues that we should put our ethnographies on trial. He imagines that a court has called him to take on the legitimacy of his findings, has put on trial his "reader's right to a reasonably reliable rending of the social world." In this trial, the jury will be on the lookout for two issues of concern. The first is the biggie: if the reader had additional information, would it change the findings of the piece? The second is much less egregious: if the reader had additional information, would it have no impact on the findings of the piece?

We can put these ideas to use when we deidentify people and places in our research.

To protect the privacy of the people in the research, ethnographers often change identifying details in their written reports. These changes should be made in ways that both obscures the identity of the respondents and honors their unique characteristics. These changes also must not in any way alter the findings of the research. When you change details to protect people's privacy, you must always also ask yourself if the changes you made altered the outcomes of your research.

First, it is important for the researcher to understand what subject characteristics need to be included to understand the findings. In a project about young mothers, for instance, it would not make sense to significantly alter a respondent's age or gender. Changing the age by a year or two might not matter, but it depends on the project. A 22-year old mother is probably not that different from one who is 23, but her experience of mothering is probably quite different from a 14-year old mother's. Or a 41-year old's. Changing the race and/or ethnicity of a respondent also requires consideration, particularly when the experience of being of a certain race or ethnicity is significant to the research (and some would argue that race and ethnicity are always relevant). To use the previous example, the experience of mothering might be different for a 14-year old White girl than for a 14-year old African American girl, with intervening variables of culture and privilege. Of course, it also may not. Researchers need to know their data, know what variables are key to the study and which are less important. Those less important variables can be changed to protect identity.

Essentially, any characteristic not directly relevant to the research can be changed to protect someone's identity. Descriptions of physical appearance can be used to hide a person's identity. Maybe that blond young man can be written into a redhead with a beard. Conversely, any characteristic that would be obvious to people in the community being researched should be changed. While we want to ensure that we have written the most authentic representation possible, we must balance that with our participants' rights to privacy. If one of your respondents is missing his right hand, people who know him well could recognize him if that is included in the narrative. Is the missing hand important to the research? If the research is about amputees, then yes, it probably is. If the research is about natural gas drilling activism, the missing hand may be irrelevant, and there is probably no need to even mention it. If relevant, perhaps 'disabled' might be an adequate descriptor, but not if that too would allow the respondent to be recognized.

We never want to erase a person's identity constructs unless there is a compelling reason to do so—and violation of confidentiality agreements are certainly compelling. No one said ethics were easy.

When changes like this are made, the reader should be alerted to the change. This can easily be done with a statement such as, 'identifying characteristics have been changed to protect privacy,' and most readers will understand this need.

Place names and locations can also be changed to protect privacy. This is often done by widening the geographic area in which the study was conducted. If I conducted a study in Aubrey, a small town in North Texas, people who live there will probably be able to identify each other when they read the report. I could just say that the study was done in North Texas, or even in Texas if the fact that it was North Texas didn't matter to the research. Or I could make up a new name for the town. If a respondent and I met at a coffee shop where she works as a barista, I could change that in the narrative to a restaurant where she waits tables.

Many ethnographers use a technique called member checking to ensure that the changes they made to protect someone's privacy didn't change the findings of the research. To do this, show the participant your writing about them and ask them if it is an accurate portrayal. I once wrote about a woman's experience as a health activist and she mentioned in an interview with me problems that she had had with a particular institution. While I had changed details about her, I mentioned the type of institution in my discussion about what happened to her. When she read the piece, she said my naming the type of institution (and I'm being intentionally vague even in this example) would reveal her identity to some readers. I disagreed—the connection seemed farfetched to me—but then who was I to say she was wrong? That part of the narrative was not instrumental to my point. I had plenty of other examples I could use to illustrate my argument, so I simply cut that example and included a different one. The participant expressed concern and I wanted to honor her feelings. In the end, the change in no way changed the outcomes of the research, and she was confident her identity could not be discerned.

It is easy to think that your participants (or people who know them) will never read your work, but your work may be more accessible than your realize (Ellis, 2009). Some of the people who took part in your ethnography will be eager to read what you wrote about them. We cannot hide behind esoteric journals and think we don't have to worry about the ethics of representation. Our goal bears repeating: we want to write the most authentic representation possible while also protecting the privacy of our research participants.

33

Write It Up

1. Think about one individual in your research. Write about how you would maintain that person's privacy while still maintaining authenticity.
2. How might you engage in member checking in your own research? What advantages and drawbacks do you see to this approach?

CHAPTER 8

TYPES OF TALES

Positivistic classification schemes are difficult to avoid, as they are so entrenched in the social sciences, and in this chapter I review one such a scheme to demonstrate some of the varieties of ethnographic writing. Van Maanen (2011) delineates a number of forms ethnographic writing may take. These types, like many classificatory schemes, overlap and may appear in different sections of one document, but they are nonetheless useful for thinking about how to frame your own narratives.

These types of writing also reflect trends and changes of fashion within the field of ethnography. While it is beyond the scope of this book, many of these forms of writing have been influenced by larger debates surrounding epistemologies and issues of representation. It is worthwhile for ethnographers to be familiar with this particular academic conversation and to consider how your own work is both influenced by and situated in these debates.

REALIST TALES

The writer of a realist tale attempts to assume an objective, omnipotent stance in the portrayal of their narrative. The realist tale has what Van Maanen (2011: 46) refers to as an "institutional voice," with a focus solely on what the research proclaims is the 'goings on' of the group under study. The piece may take on a documentary tone, with a lot of focus on mundane details to support various points that the author wants to make. Written in third person, the 'I' of the author is not present in the narrative, nor is there any discussion of researcher subjectivity. Historically, this style of writing up results was used to justify the 'science' of ethnography (and more general, of the social sciences). Tapping into the ethos that good science is exemplified by objectivity, the writer assumes a detached, god-like vantage point. When subjectivity enters the narrative, it is from the participant's point of view in the form of quotes. "The narrator," Van Maanen (2011: 53) writes, "speaks for the group studied as a passive observer who roams imperialistically across the setting to tell of events that happen in this way or that."

This type of writing has been problematized by methodologists, and should be viewed with a critical lens by ethnographers in particular due to the imperialistic roots of our chosen method. Lack of reflexivity translates to a lack of transparency on the part of the researcher. What was the researcher's motive? What biases interrupted the researcher's gaze? While there may be no malign intent on the part of the researcher, critics argue that we need to interrogate this style and explore the unsaid as well as the said. Deconstruction of objectivity in research raises questions not easily answered about the possibility of an objective stance.

With the emphasis on researchers' standpoint and reflexivity in recent decades, stand-alone realist tales have largely fallen out of fashion, although this type of tale is still the primary mode of writing quantitative research reports. On the other hand, a researcher should be cognizant that many readers have been socialized to accept this sort of writing as 'scientific.' People outside of the science debates may have trouble (if not outright hostility to) accepting narratives that deviate from the realist tale as scientific. Or even as research.

"Academics are given the 'story line' that the 'I' should be suppressed in their writing, that they should accept homogenization and adopt the all knowing, all powerful voice of the academy," Richardson (1997: 2) writes. "But contemporary philosophic thought raises problems that exceed and undermine that academic story line....We work in a highly complex period: On the one hand poststructuralism calls us to greater play, reflexivity and ethical responsibility about our writing. On the other, the institutions that hire us may adhere to older canons of writing practices."

CONFESSIONAL TALES

Confessional tales begin to lift the curtain behind the research process and help to resolve some of the issues raised when we problematize realist tales. In this sort of tale, the researcher has a presence in the narrative. The writer explains how he or she went about conducting the research, and includes discussion of researcher standpoint, bias, and subjectivity. The reader follows the fieldworker through the journey of discovery in the narrative. The character of the fieldworker is developed in the story along with those of the participants.

Through this journey, the reader learns from the author the hows and whys of the project. The author answers questions such as why the researcher chose this particular field for study. How did the researcher gain access to and navigate within the group? What did they consider data, and how did they analyze that data? The confessional tale uses a blending of information about the findings of the project along with insights into the process of the project.

IMPRESSIONIST/LITERARY TALES

Impressionist writers cast off the omnipotence of realist or confessional tales and draw the reader into a dramatic story. Utilizing literary and creative nonfiction techniques, writers of this type of tale strive to present compelling stories that draw in readers. Characters are developed, and their stories are presented with a literary structure. The writing may read like a novel, ripe with thick description and character development. These are stories, provocative, engaging, and difficult for the reader to put down. This type of tale incorporates the transparency of the confessional tale with extensive use of creative nonfiction.

Literary tales push the impressionist style further. They may even be written as fiction (Gullion, 2014; Leavy, 2015). Techniques of fiction are used to tell the story, and the pacing is similar to that of a novel rather than a research report.

My own social fiction novel, *October Birds*, is a fictional account of how public health would likely respond to a large-scale public health disaster, based in research.

I chose fiction as a mode of representation for that project for three reasons. First, through fiction, I could draw on the totality of my experiences—the researcher as embodied research. I have significant experience researching community responses to health threats. I also have practical experience working in these types of situations—prior to becoming a college professor, I had a career as the Chief Epidemiologist at one of the largest health departments in Texas. I have amassed a significant body of research and I have years of hands-on work on disease outbreaks and natural disasters. I have all this expertise and knowledge in my head, information that could help people in a disaster situation. Through fiction I could draw on the entirety of this reservoir, rather than simply focusing on whatever research project I'm currently involved in.

The second reason I chose to write a novel is the breadth of the potential audience. We all know what most journal articles are read by only a handful of people. Through fiction, I had the opportunity to engage in public scholarship.

Finally, I used fiction as an educational platform. Health education campaigns employ a variety of strategies to raise health literacy, and I see my novel as contributing to that. Most people have little contact with public health—when public health works, the public shouldn't see it. The water is clean, there aren't any outbreaks of deadly infectious diseases, and people are healthy. I wanted to write a book that would allow people to see behind the scenes so that when they do encounter public health they can better understand how disease control works.

In the novel then, I drew on the totality of my experiences as a researcher, teacher, public health professional, and artist to create a scenario that I hoped would both resonate with the general public and inform them about what would likely happen in the case of a pandemic. This type of ethnographic writing blurs academic and lay realms. While a work of fiction, *October Birds* is grounded in sociological and public health research, and much of what happens in the novel are based on real events.

CRITICAL/ADVOCACY TALES

Many ethnographers hold an ethic of social justice and see their work as a form of activism. Critical tales are written with a social change agenda. They shed light on some problem in society, some trouble in need of fixing. The advocacy tale carries this a step further, with a clear social change agenda. Not only are the problems unveiled, but the author presents solutions as well. Through this approach, the writer clearly attempts to give back to the community involved in the research. The text is more than a report on a social issue, but advocates directly for solutions.

This type of tale is diametrically opposed to the attempted objective stance of the realist tale. The author takes a firm position on an issue and the piece is written with the intent of spurring readers to take a particular action in the name of social change.

COLLABORATIVE TALES

Collaborative tales are becoming increasingly common as a means to dismantle the research/researched hierarchy. In this style, the researcher and one or more participants jointly write the narrative. Collaborative writing is a response to the violence of knowledge appropriation as well as the imperialism we discussed earlier.

Collaborative writers want to ensure that the people involved in their project have a clear voice in the outcome, that the experience of participation in the project was just as beneficial to the participants as it was to the researcher. They consider issues of language and literacy, and the need to communicate clearly. So many articles are written in an academese that is inaccessible to most people (sometimes even to fellow academics). Collaborative writers ask who creates and who consumes knowledge, and are the outcomes of knowledge generation equitable to all parties involved?

LeCompte and Schensul (2013: 281) suggest writing using the narrative forms that the group you are studying uses. "Some researchers," they write, "argue that presenting non-Western ideas in a Western format destroys their meaning." While this may be true, I encourage you to approach this technique with caution, and consider whether or not writing in indigenous forms is cultural appropriation. Smith (2012: 2) writes that "most indigenous peoples and their communities do not differentiate scientific or 'proper' research from forms of amateur collecting, journalistic approaches, film making or other ways of 'taking' indigenous knowledge." Ethically, researchers must be cognizant of issues of power, justice, and colonialism in their work, and writing is no exception.

Your safest bet in this case is collaborative writing with members of the group.

On the other hand, if you choose to take on collaborative writing, you must also ensure that collaboration involves "authentic participation" (Savin-Badin & Major, 2013: 217) from the community you researched, that you are not simply giving lip service to the process. In a true collaboration, all of the authors should have equal voice in not only the crafting of the document but also in the final written work. This involves a significant loss of control on the part of the researcher (Gullion & Ellis, 2013).

POST-STRUCTURALIST AND EXPERIMENTAL TALES

Ethnographies should not be limited in form, and ethnographic writers play with a number of different experimental techniques to represent their work. Perhaps the opposite of the realist tale is the experimental tale. In this tale, reality is conceived as mutable. The story is open-ended, and may use a number of experimental writing forms. The uncertainty inherent in human life is brought to the forefront.

Margaret Sommerville's beautiful ethnography, *Water in a Dry Land* (2013), is a compelling example of how to write an alternative to traditional academic narratives. This ethnography is not only about water, but it wants to *be* water.

In the text, Sommerville considered the mutual entanglements of natural and human-made ecosystems, and the crisis of unsustainable water practices. Her writing ebbs and flows like the water systems she describes. She writes that "each time a story, an artwork, or a piece of writing was produced constituted a pause, a temporary stopping place in an iterative process of representation and reflection. In this way, each instance of representation did not aim at stasis but has its own truth in which meaning is formed relationally, dynamically, and intertextually." In this way we as readers flow through her ethnography.

As you can see, there are a number of possibilities when it comes to textual representations of your ethnographic work. You are encouraged to explore them further and find what forms best speak to your own work. You may also want to consider writing your ethnography in different forms to see how the selection of textual style influences the piece. This also allows you different avenues for publication—perhaps for one journal you write your results as an impressionistic piece, while for another you write an ethnodrama based off your work. While beyond the scope of this text, you might also want to consider nontextual, arts-based representations, such as visual art, photography, or dance.

Write It Up

1. Intentionally write one scene from your research in at least three of the different types of tales described above. Which best represented that particular scene?
2. Choose the type of tale that resonates most with you. Defend it to its detractors.

REFLEXIVITY

As I mentioned above, realist tales are problematic because they ignore the issue of researcher subjectivity. In recent decades, a hallmark of qualitative research has become the inclusion of researcher reflexivity in the written account of the research.

Through reflexive practice, researchers continually interrogate their own standpoints in relation to the subject matter under research. Through reflexive engagement, we ask "how much of the researcher is in the research" (Savin-Badin & Major, 2013: 69). To what extent do our own backgrounds and experiences influence the research?

I find that when students practice reflexivity, the difficulty comes in where and how much to write that practice into the text. With the emphasis on reflexivity, how do we position ourselves in our stories? And an added concern, how do we balance transparency without becoming intrusive? As Westbrook (2008: 112) notes, "a reflexive stance does not guarantee the quality of ethnographic writing... 'know thyself' can all too easily be heard, especially in an insecure and therapeutic age, as 'become self-centered, indulgent, snippy.'" He continues: "Given both the intellectual dangers inherent in reflexivity and the centrality of the navigator/author, considerable discipline is required in order to prevent egotism, or merely self-indulgence, from overwhelming the expression of an ethnography."

Despite Westbook's concerns, reflexivity is an important piece of your narrative. Hopefully, you have engaged in reflexive practice throughout your fieldwork, a practice in which researchers "interrogate their deeply held beliefs that become apparent in undertaking research" (Savin-Badin & Major, 2013: 69). Through discussion of researcher reflexivity, we demonstrate that we have thought about how we as researchers contributed to the outcome of the research, how our standpoint influences our decision-making, how the process unfolded, and how we interpreted and made sense and meanings out of the data.

Savin-Badin and Major (2013: 76) recommend we examine three major areas in which our personal stance could influence the outcome of our research: (1) In relation to the subject matter, (2) In relation to the participants, and (3) In relation to the research context and process. Everything about who we are as individuals could lead us in certain directions, whether it be our demographics (race, gender, social class, sexuality, language, and so forth), or our past experiences, or our moral and ethical worldview, who we are as individuals plays into our academic work. "It is not possible to remain outside the subject or process of the research and look in," they write, "rather, the researcher is both integral and integrated into the research."

I'm often asked how to represent this in the text, and perhaps more often, where to place reflexivity in one's narrative. In some cases, delineating a separate standpoint section might fit well with the literary flow of the work. This could include a subheading, and often makes logical sense to include alongside your discussion of method. In a more standalone literary style, a discreet reflexivity section might be awkward. In this case, many writers make use of the abstract or a preface for this purpose. Others integrate clues about researcher subjectivity throughout the story. This is an example of what I mean:

> "We'd been staking out this shooting gallery for months," Officer Gonzales said.
>
> I must have had a puzzled look on my face. I assumed we weren't talking about a gun range or a carnival game. "Shooting gallery?" I asked.
>
> "You've heard of a crack house, right?" she said. "It's like that, a house where they go to buy heroin and shoot it up. Sometimes we find needles in the yard, right were kids could touch them. It's disgusting."

Without being explicit about her lack of knowledge of this aspect of heroin culture, the researcher clues the reader that this is her first encounter with this use of the term 'shooting gallery.' By using this sort of textual clue, the reader learns about the background and experience of the researcher, yet the flow of the narrative isn't interrupted with heavy-handed reflexive interjections. Weaving information into the story in this manner may also protect the writer from some of the criticisms of those who misunderstand the role of reflexivity and label it narcissistic navel-gazing (Sparkes, 2002).

Reflexive positioning helps to establish credibility. In the above example, we learn that the researcher did not hold expertise about heroin users going into the project. Officer Gonzales, however, does. Thus, the officer is set up in the story as a credible source, both knowledgeable and experienced when it comes to this topic. The researcher doesn't need to be the expert in this instance, because the officer holds that role. The officer's knowledge is shared with the reader through the use of quotes.

If you have the space (and this may be more likely in a book-length manuscript than in a journal article) and it suits the flow of your story, you might consider including a section on evaluating narrative ethnography. Discuss how this type of work is assessed by other professionals in the field and note how your work meets those criteria. This will help people not familiar with this type of work to evaluate its contribution to the scholarly conversation. While it can be frustrating to have to defend your work in this manner, it is unfortunately true that we are constantly judged as scholars (this is, of course, not limited to ethnography, but is the case throughout academia).

Including reflexive statements also gives the reader tools with which to evaluate the work. As many social researchers were schooled in positivism, new ethnographers often worry their work will be judged on variables more appropriate for quantitative research, such as validity, reliability, bias, N-size, and so forth. Because colleagues less familiar with qualitative writing are likely to judge your work (for example, when you apply for jobs or go up for tenure), you can give them the tools to judge your work on *your terms* in your writing, rather than relying on theirs. Just as you brought biases to your ethnographic research, others will bring biases to the reading of your work.

AUDIENCE

I've mentioned your reader a number of times so far in this book, so let's take a moment to look at who those readers are. Audience matters. When writing, we should have a pretty good idea of who is in our intended audience and we should write for them. Audience should influence our writing style. I write differently when addressing undergraduate students than I do to subject matter experts because our shared understanding of the material is different. I write differently to my children than I do to college students for the same reason. As an author, you don't want to frustrate or alienate your reader. Because guess what? They'll probably stop reading. Writing clear, understandable prose allows your reader to connect with your material. "Because all writing is socially situated," Golden-Biddle and Locke (2007: 3) remind us, "social scientists should have particular audiences and purposes in mind when they write."

Through narrative structures—through story-telling—we can disseminate our information broadly. Making your work accessible both to scholarly audiences and to those who would benefit from your work, who *need* this work, is not always easy. We tend to be trained to write in a discipline-explicit manner. Hence the Ivory-tower criticism of much academic writing. To reach a broader audience, we must learn to explain complex social phenomena clearly and concisely.

When writing ethnography, I typically envision three main audiences. The first is comprised of subject-matter experts in the topics I present— other academics in my field. This group already has in-depth knowledge of the literature and comes to the text well prepared to engage with my ideas. Termed 'collegial readers' by Van Maanen (2011), this group includes your immediate colleagues. For these readers, jargon and citations work to position your work as part of the ongoing conversation about whatever particular topic you are writing about. "Used carefully," Van Mannen (2011: 27–28) writes, "these terms and phrases convey fairly stable, technical, and precise meanings to knowledgeable readers and help locate a text, and more importantly, the writer, within a given tradition of ethnographic practice and interest."

The danger of jargon, of course, is that it can be either used incorrectly, without comprehensive understanding of the meanings of the terms, or that jargon can be used as an 'exclusionary tool' (Van Maanen, 2011), that alienates the uninitiated. The Body without Organs has specific meaning to a particular group of scholars. For the uninitiated, the phrase will likely be glossed over, or worse, may cause the reader to put down the text.

The second audience I think about is comprised of educated non-experts. This group is made up primarily of academics (graduate students and faculty), from a variety of disciplines. Also well prepared to engage with the text and used to academic writing, some concepts and technical details will nonetheless be unfamiliar to them. Academic and other experts outside your field look to your work for specific information about the people, and/or activities they engage in, that your study presents. Many of these readers are looking for background information that will bolster their own work. They may look to you for details to include in their own literature reviews, or to use your research as data in their own social activism. As Van Maanen (2011: 31) notes, "Ethnographies are looked to for facts surrounding low visibility, little-understood, deviant, or otherwise out-of-the-ordinary cultures."

The final audience is the cross-over lay public. This audience is the least familiar with academic texts but has an interest in the topic I'm writing about. I tend to think of this group as people who are educated but not necessarily educated on my particular topic. They read for general interest in the subject and may have no background, technically or otherwise, in this field. Writing to this group should be relatively jargon-free and written in accessible, quality language. Some terms may need explanation. While the collegial reader may understand what "ethnography" means, for example, the lay reader would likely benefit from a brief explanation of what you mean by the term.

An academic writing tone tends to appeal most to the first group, while a narrative storytelling approach tends to appeal most to the third group. For the second group (the group I generally write for), blending academic writing and storytelling is the best vehicle for engagement. I can thus, for example, tell these readers a definition, and also show them what that word looks like through a story. I want my writing to engage directly with largest potential audience, while remaining accessible to both of the other groups.

Ultimately, however, I am writing for myself, writing something that I would enjoy reading.

Our writing should include whatever disciplinary cues are needed to ensure that readers will find it credible. Van Maanen (2011: 29) argues that "an ethnography should be empirical enough to be credible and analytical enough to be interesting." In my discipline of sociology, this typically means that I should provide a thorough discussion of what specific techniques I employed. This is an example of how to write that up from my book, *Fracking the Neighborhood* (Gullion, 2015):

> Primary data included both fieldwork and in-depth interviews (typically lasting one to three hours) with twenty key players in the drilling debate in the Barnett Shale. These were leaders publicly identifiable as persons active in the protest of natural gas drilling in their communities. They regularly speak at public meetings. They produce reports for city officials and other entities. Most of the activists maintain blogs and/or Facebook groups dedicated to the opposition of drilling in the Barnett Shale. I also had the opportunity to interview some of the regulatory officials involved, both at the local and state level.

> I also attended grassroots organizational meetings, 'town hall' style meetings hosted by regulatory agencies (such as the Environmental Protection Agency and the Texas Commission on Environmental Quality), municipal and county oil and gas taskforce meetings, and city council meetings. I attended and participated in protests and rallies. I had numerous informal, instrumental conversations with people at these events. I wrote detailed field notes following each meeting, event, or interview I participated in. In the field notes I worried less about what people were saying and more about the actions that happened, and I relied on digital recordings to accurately transcribe what was said. I kept a running file of field notes and interspersed them with extensive memo writing.

> I visited several sites with active natural gas drilling operations in order to better understand how the proximity of drilling might impact residents. As an example, one home I visited was in the center of three natural gas pad sites. Two of the sites were within 500 feet of the home and a third site was 200 feet from the home. One of the pads was fitted with a diesel-fueled compressor that ran twenty-four hours per day, and made a loud, clanging noise that could be heard inside the house.

> Secondary data included news articles, reports generated by regulatory agencies, websites (including those from governmental and regulatory agencies and from grassroots organizations), scientific reports, blogs,

and open-access online discussion groups. All secondary data that I used is publically available.

Finally, I draw on what St. Pierre (2011: 621) terms "transgressive data":

emotional data, dream data, sensual data, memory data, and *response data*—data that were not visible and that disrupted linearity, consciousness, and the mind/body dichotomy. Much data—*what we think when we think about a topic*—were identified *during* analysis and not before. Until one begins to think, one cannot know what one will think with. In that sense, data are collected during thinking and... especially during writing. (italics in original)

I gained entrance into the activist and regulatory groups by being a fixture at different meetings, a constant presence. I asked informal questions during the actions and had informal conversations with people in attendance. Over time I grew to know some of the key players who then introduced me to others. During formal interviews, I spoke with people in depth about their experience in a narrative fashion, with most of the interviews starting from the simple question, "Tell me your story, how did you get involved?" and progressing forward in a participant-led discussion.

These facts (you will notice there are a lot of quantitative descriptors here) lend credence to my knowledge claims due to the sheer volume of information analyzed. In the selection, you may have also noticed a few statements that might draw a reader's interest aside from the empiricism. For example, the statements, "Two of the sites were within 500 feet of the home and a third site was 200 feet from the home. One of the pads was fitted with a diesel-fueled compressor that ran twenty-four hours per day, and made a loud, clanging noise that could be heard inside the house," provide descriptive information to draw a reader into the story behind the data.

The detail of the "loud, clanging noise that could be heard inside the house" is compelling. A reader can imagine themselves in that space, imagine sitting inside their home and hearing a loud, clanging noise coming in from industrial activity outside. The reader can image 200 feet, and realize that is very close to a home.

I recently coauthored an article on the application of Latour's Actor-Network Theory (ANT) to piracy off the coast of Somalia (Gullion & Gullion, 2015). A subject-matter expert in ANT should readily understand Latour's theory with little explanation, and when writing to that audience, my coauthor and I could quickly mention the theoretical framework and delve directly into its application to piracy. That expert should be able to follow our argument readily. Members of the second audience, educated non-experts, may require more explanation and background of ANT before they could follow our argument. While writing with that audience in mind, we need to explain some of the more technical jargon. The cross-over lay audience, well, they're more likely here for the pirates than for the actor-network theory. To capture (and maintain) their interest, we could balance the theoretical aspects of the paper with pirate narratives. As you can see, knowing which audience you are writing to can have a significant impact on what you write.

SECTION II

NARRATIVE STRUCTURES

STORY ARCS

At some point in your writing, you need to take a step back from the details of your tale and consider the overall structure of the piece. You want to make sure that in its entirety the tale not only makes logical sense, but also that you get across the meanings you want to convey. Previously, I discussed types of ethnographic tales—now we want to consider both the structure of the whole work and the details that bring cohesion to the overall piece.

By structure, I'm referring to the architecture, or 'blue prints' of your piece (Hart, 2011). This is somewhat different from an outline of the project. Rather than simply thinking that A happens, followed by B and C, we want to think about how the reader *gets* from A to C, how you will *carry your reader through* the story to the end.

Part of the beauty of ethnography is the unfolding of events in the field, the transformations that bloom in the course of the project. Our written work should be dynamic as well, to capture that flow. As fieldworkers, we spend a significant length of time in the field researching. Stuff happens. Our writing should reflect that movement. The ethnographer who presents events as static categories belies this beauty. Narayan (2012: 13) writes that "the situation [that we research] might include the site of the fieldwork, various personal circumstances, the historical and social moment, and even prevailing theories about the subject of research. The story, though, follows the transformations—physical, emotional, intellectual—that an ethnographer experiences personally or witnesses in others." We want to present that story.

One way to approach this is to think about the plot of your story, just as we would think about plot in fiction or TV shows or movies. Golden-Biddle and Locke (2007: 4) write about plot in ethnographic writing as a "theorized storyline." Thinking of the trajectory of the plot line in our own tales, we can work to ensure that we engage our readers and carry them through to the end of our stories. The narrative structure of the story arc fits well with this approach. This is in juxtaposition to "the predominant style of writing that we find in journal articles as unadorned and disembodied, with the experience nature of writing as a complex process of creating knowledge" (2007: 10).

The proliferation of unadorned and disembodied writing style stems from the reification of science as epistemology, with 'science' often conceived in very narrow terms. We want to do something better than bore our readers with unadorned facts. We want to tell them the story of what happened in the field, to theorize, to draw our readers into a new world, into a new way of seeing the familiar. We want them to hate the idea of putting our book down, and to remember and refer to (and cite!) our work long after they've finished reading it.

In this chapter, we will take a look at the nuts and bolts of how to organize your text into a plot line. As I mentioned earlier, good stories contain relatable characters who desire something and who must overcome obstacles to try to get it (Hart, 2011). This is the essence of good story telling. Maybe the characters get what they desire, maybe not, but there is some sort of resolution, some main point that the reader gains from having accompanied you on this journey. This journey is what's known as a story arc, a path through your story.

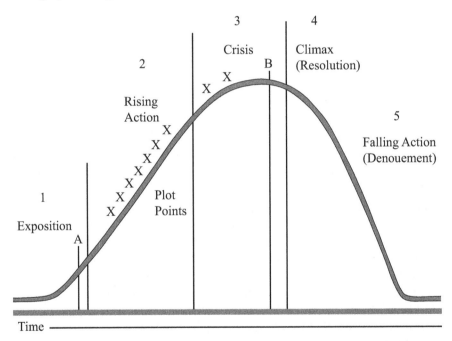

Figure 3. A story arc
(Source: Hart, 2011: 25)

Story arcs have a beginning, a middle, and an end (although they need not be written or presented in that order). We can visualize our arc as a bell curve skewed slightly to the left. Or more poetically, as a wave of action set to break. Hart (2011) breaks down five major areas within that curve that we must attend to in order to lead our reader through our tales: (1) Exposition, (2) Rising Action, (3) Crisis, (4) Climax (Resolution), and (5) Falling Action (Denouement). Plot points—events that alter the trajectory of the action—occur along the way.

This arc is present in nearly all good stories, whether fiction or nonfiction. Deconstruct the stories that you enjoy and you will find this underlying structure—in fact, in making this a practice, you can begin to understand what works and what doesn't in the stories you consume, and apply those lessons to your own writing.

Hart (2011: 10) writes, "A plot emerges when a storyteller carefully selects and arranges material so that larger meanings can emerge." This emergent structure is what we as ethnographers strive for. While we want to convey the specifics of our particular research setting, we are also, as social scientists, looking for larger meanings, for understandings that resonate and connect with people outside of the groups we study. If we can't accomplish this, our work is at risk of degrading into fetishism and othering of an outside group.

In the first stage of the arc—exposition—we introduce the reader to the world of our ethnographic research. Here we present the characters to the reader and give whatever background information that the reader has to have to understand what is about to happen. As this is an ethnographic study, the history of the community you worked in is part of that exposition. Hart cautions us though not to reveal too much too soon. Pages and pages that set up the story are boring. The main point to keep in mind (and the italics are here for a reason) is that you should give the reader the *minimum* background information necessary to move forward into the story. We don't have to give all the detail up front. Expository details can be woven into the narrative. Blending exposition with action gives the reader fine points of information without weighing down your story. Remember, readers like for something to happen. We want action.

We can also pull readers into our story with some foreshadowing within our exposition. For example:

Jenny didn't know anything was wrong with her newborn. She held his slick, just-born body against her chest and whispered, 'hello.'

These two sentences provide expository detail. A woman named Jenny has just given birth to a son. The passage also draws the reader into the story, teasing the reader with a big unanswered question: What is wrong with the baby?

After some (brief) exposition, we move into the next area of the story arc, which Hart calls rising action. Something needs to happen. The story is spun in some direction with the use of plot points. Remember here that you want to capitalize on the dynamic nature of your ethnographic work. A tornado rips the roof off the house. A woman finds a lump in her breast. A student points a handgun at his instructor. Your protagonist (your participant) is confronted with some sort of problem or challenge that requires action:

> "We need to talk about the spring," [my department chair] said.

> Next spring would be my last semester as a graduate student; I planned on teaching and finishing up my dissertation. I was going to give birth in February, defend my dissertation in April, and graduate in May. Some of the other graduate teaching assistants had recently told me they'd already received their teaching assignments for the spring. I was currently the senior among them, and it was a general policy that seniority equated better classes. This fall I was teaching research methods and statistics, and so I assumed I would teach them again.

> "I can't hire you as a GTA in the spring since you are pregnant," she said. "It would be too disruptive to have you leave in the middle of the semester." She picked some lint off her sweater, flicked it on the floor, and stared at me. (Gullion, 2008)

Your protagonist is confronted with a problem. And not just one problem or challenge. There may be several plot points, several times that a person or group is knocked off their trajectory. Hart depicts this as a rising oscillation, perhaps of hope (it's raised, it's crushed, it's raised again), or mystery (we learn a bit more and a bit more about what is going on), or suspense.

Constructing a feeling of tension in our readers helps to pull them along through your narrative. Ellis (2009: 304) sums this up in her own writing: "I seek to take readers into the immediacy of particular scenes, dramatic action, vivid conversation, and forward-moving plots." We want our readers to keep reading so they can find out what happens next. I know that sounds like an onerous task, but when we integrate literary devices into our writing we can build the sort of tension that keeps readers reading.

When we pay attention to the pacing, or forward movement of our story, we can help ensure that our readers remained engaged. We portray that movement when we use action verbs. Remember that stuff needs to happen in your story. Hart (2011: 119) writes that "a story is a journey, and journeys can be tedious or fascinating." I suspect that as academics, we can all readily identify examples of tedious journeys in academic writing. Be honest, how many times have you skipped through sections of a journal article out of sheer boredom? I've done it more often than I'd like to admit. Which is really kind of sad for those authors if you think about it. They probably spent hours and hours writing that paper, and all I read is the introduction and the conclusion. If that.

Pacing involves the speed at which the action in your story happens. We can alternate the pace—moving quickly through less relevant bits and slowing down the action during the more important scenes. As you read your own work, notice points you want to skip hurriedly through (I realize no one wants to admit this about their own work, but try it out). When that happens, revise that section to speed up the pace. Use action verbs to get the reader through the dull bits faster (ergo transforming the dull bits into interesting bits).

A classic literary device for building tension is the cliff hanger. Set up a tense scene and then jump to another part of the story, leaving the readers to wait a few moments for how that cliff-hanger will resolve. A good place to do this is at the end of a major section or chapter. "You don't need to create literal cliff-hangers—Indiana Jones dangling from a sapling on a vertical face high above a river," Hart (2011: 32–33) writes, "but you do want to close out each little episode with a kicker that leaves your protagonist, and your audience, dangling." We can also make sure that we parcel out information and not give the readers the conclusion too soon. Give the reader time to imagine what is going to happen next and how the story will end; most readers enjoy a pleasant surprise when what they've imagined is not quite what happens (hence the success of novels like *Gone Girl*).

Tension builds and culminates in the third section of our arc: the crisis. At the moment of crisis, "everything hangs in the balance" (Hart, 2011: 34). Events could fall for or against the protagonist. Buffy and the vampire have each other by the throats—one will die and one will live. Your audience is poised in a collectively held breath—everything written so far has built up to this moment. Your hero(s) will either triumph or be crushed: "The crisis is the peak of the breaking wave, the wave's force will change things profoundly" (Hart, 2011: 36).

The wave crests in climax, our fourth area in the narrative arc. The climax resolves the crisis. All of the tension that has built up until this point releases: We learn the outcome.

As the climax resolves, our story arc dissolves into falling action. We tie up loose ends. Like the exposition at the onset of our tale, we want to "wrap things up as quickly as possible and leave the stage" (Hart, 2011: 39). Most people don't enjoy long, drawn out endings. Tie it up and go.

Hart suggests, and I agree, that you end you tale with a kicker, a line or phrase that locks up your story, yet leaves your reader wanting more. Editorial writers often employ this technique, and it works well. Here's an example from my book, *Fracking the Neighborhood*:

> As I was finishing this manuscript, activists in the city of Denton won a significant victory in their fight against urban natural gas activities, and Denton become the first city in Texas to ban hydraulic fracturing.
>
> A grassroots organization called the Denton Drilling Awareness Group amassed thousands of signatures on a petition calling for a ballot measure to ban fracking within the city limits. In November of 2014 the ban was put to a vote, in which it prevailed overwhelmingly despite an intensive pro-industry campaign. One pro-drilling organization, Denton Taxpayers, purportedly spent about $700,000 fighting the measure, using funds largely donated by natural gas companies (Heinkel-Wolfe, 2014).
>
> In response to the outcome of the vote, the Texas Railroad Commissioner said that "he was disappointed that voters 'fell prey to scare tactics and mischaracterizations of the truth in passing the hydraulic fracturing ban'" (Baker, 2014). Denton's mayor, on the other hand, defended the voters' choice and proclaimed that the city would "exercise the legal remedies that are available to us should the ordinance be challenged" (Baker, 2014).
>
> While passing the ban, the voters of Denton also elected a slate of Republican candidates into office.
>
> A lawsuit challenging the ban was filed by noon the day after the vote.

The book ends with a kicker that indicates that the story is not over.

Write It Up

1. Map your ethnography onto a graph of the story arc. Identify each element under the curve within your tale.
2. Write a kicker for the ending of your own project.

CHAPTER 12

VOICE

Ethnographers have two sets of voices to contend with. The first is the researcher's voice—that is, how our own voice comes across on the page. The second set of voices are those of the participants in our ethnography. We need to consider both how we capture and represent their unique voices, so that they sound separate from our own. Since we potentially have a multitude of voices speaking throughout our tale, we don't ever want our reader to question who is speaking and have to hunt for an answer. Let's explore the researcher's voice first.

Anton Chekhov said, "There are big dogs and little dogs, but little dogs must not fret over the existence of the big ones. Everyone is obligated to howl in the voice that the Lord God has given him" (as quoted in Narayan, 2012: 86). Our writing voice is our howl.

Voice is, quite literally, the voice in the reader's head as he or she reads your words. When considering voice, we want to give our readers "a personable companion who's going to bring some humanity to the experience" (Hart, 2011: 64). Voice is the person who is telling the story, whether it is written in first, second, or third person. It is you—your personality, your quirks, your style—textually embodied. When people read our work, our voice occupies their minds for a period of time. Voice is the 'me' that comes through my writing, the intonations that these black squiggles on the page make in your brain as you scan them.

But do *you* come across in your writing? Likewise, is your voice one that people will want to listen to for however many pages you take to make your argument?

I try to write like I talk (although I strive for a bit more eloquence, and without all the 'ums' and 'likes' and wild hand gestures). Try this: read your work out loud. Listen. Does it sound like you? Sometimes we worry so much about getting our words right—about polishing and editing—that we revise our voice right out of the text. Or worse, we let an editor revise away our voice.

Hart (2011: 73) has some great advice on this. "The ultimate secret to letting your voice sound on the page is simply to relax and be yourself." He continues: "A relaxed writer is a fast writer, and fast writers sound more like themselves…writers who agonize over a rough draft, futzing with every word, will submerge their true selves in nondescript formality."

I have found one of the best ways to stop that futzing is to set a daily word count and hold myself to it. I got this idea from the creators of NaNoWriMo (National Novel Writing Month). NaNoWriMo challenges authors to write a 50,000 word novel in 30 days (that's a book about the size of this one). The best way to accomplish this is to divide the word count into writing 1667 words per day.

That's a lot of words. A frenzy of writing. And you probably aren't going to write all those words until you slay your inner editor.

What is your inner editor? That's the part of you that futzes over every word that you type. The part of you that sits in front of the computer watching the cursor flash and tries to mentally compose the perfect sentence. To write 1667 words per day though, you don't have time for that. You've got other things to do! NaNoWriMo is in November. It's the start of the holiday season! There's turkey to cook and school events to attend and work to do and people to see.

It can be done though, and every year people manage to finish. I wrote my first novel, *October Birds* (2014), during a NaNoWriMo using this very technique. Once I accepted the fact that I had to just write, I found the practice liberating. Just write. You can always edit later. In fact, later you will want to futz over your words, your structure, your narrative arc—all of those details. But first you have to get the words on the page. And when you approach your writing this way, when you slay your inner editor and let your words spill out of you, your unique voice will howl and howl.

If you want to be a fast, relaxed writer, you need to give your inner editor something else to do. She can come back later when you've written your piece and you are ready to edit it. She'll love that, and she'll have a sharpened pencil at the ready when it's time. But for now, give her a kitten or something else to play with. Whenever she tries to interrupt your work, tell her, "I don't need you now, but I will later. I still have a thousand words to write. Leave me alone."

Write It Up

1. Write 1667 words today about your project. Don't look at your notes and don't over-think the process. Leave all mistakes alone. Just write.
2. Practice letting go of your inner editor. Set a timer for fifteen minutes and free-write about your research. Every time you try to edit yourself, write the words, "I don't have time to edit now, I will edit later," and then continue writing.

ACADEMIC FAN FICTION

I wrote my first book at age 9. With what I thought were clever, subtle plot revisions, I ripped off Walter Farley's novel, *Flame*. Captivated by a subterranean passageway to a hidden world (of horses no less!), I got to live in that world not only while reading but also in retelling my own version of the story (in mine the protagonist was a girl and the horse, a filly).

As a genre, fan fiction emerged with the same sensibility: How could people continue to be part of these exceptional fictional worlds? To keep the story going after the author has written the last page?

This got me wondering. Could we write academic fan nonfiction? I always ask my students to list their favorite authors (of any genre) in class. What do you like about those works? What do the authors do well? Examine the stylistic cues. For example, Robert Sullivan (as cited in Bennett, 2010: 6) describes mundane objects so poetically, I ruminate over his words long after I read his descriptions. In this passage, he poetically describes a garbage dump:

> There had been rain the night before, so it wasn't long before I found a little leachette seep, a black ooze trickling down the slope of the hill, an espresso of refuse... this little seep was pure pollution, a pristine stew of oil and grease, of cyanide and arsenic, of cadmium, chromium, copper, lead, nickel, silver, mercury, and zinc. I touched this fluid—my fingertip was a bluish caramel color—and it was warm and fresh. A few yards away, where the stream collected into a benzene-scented pool, a mallard swam alone.

An "espresso of refuse"? It would have been sufficient for Sullivan to write that the dump site was polluted—but instead he portrays the site as something both beautiful and deadly. I'd like to emulate this type of detail and pace in my own writing.

Gore (2007: 67–68) notes that many writing teachers have their students copy (by hand) the work of writers they admire. "By doing this," she argues, "you will read the entire work with new eyes and new ears. You will unlock the mystery of your master's magic. You'll peel away the paint and the plaster to discover the secret architecture that holds their stories up." Try it.

Read with an eye towards writing. And read broadly to inform your own work—both in terms of content and style. Consume not only academic books and journal articles, but also OpEds and popular nonfiction, novels, short stories, essays, poetry, plays, and comic books. Broad reading increases your vocabulary and idea base, and it exposes you to a variety of literary voices and writing styles. Your own writing voice will become more sophisticated as a result.

As we develop our own voices stylistically, we can look to auth.3ors whose work we enjoy and emulate them. And over time, our voice will evolve. It strengthens with experience and confidence. The voice of my early work is still me, but it's not the same I howl with today.

Write It Up

1. Find your favorite passage from your favorite writer. Copy it by hand.

CHAPTER 14

WRITING THE VOICES OF OUR PARTICIPANTS

Our voice is not the only voice in our ethnographies. Our participants should have voice as well, distinct from our own, with their own quicks and speech patterns—with their own howls. Since we are engaging in ethnographic practice, we also want to call on the voices of our participants; ours should not be the only voice in the tale.

This can create an interesting conundrum—should we (and to what extent) edit our participant's words?

When you were in the field you probably had an audio or video recorder with you at least part of the time. You likely have word-for-word transcripts of your participants, so you can write out their exact wording in your story. If that wording was awkward, should you change it? What about all the placeholder words, the ums and likes, should you delete those?

I recently clashed with an editor over this point. I quoted a participant thusly: "People get angry and they say things, and [I'm] just like, just present the information." The 'I'm' was not verbalized—at that point the participant paused with a nonverbal gesture. I placed the 'I'm' there in brackets because I felt it clarified his meaning.

The editor commented, "It may be better to quote verbatim here. Whatever was replaced by the bracketed word, it can hardly have been worse than 'I'm just like.'" The editor's comment made me laugh. Because, while the grammar was terrible, the quote accurately portrayed how this individual speaks.

We never want to embarrass our participants in the reflection of their words. "Speech itself is a status indicator," Hart (2011: 86) reminds us. I once showed a participant an article I was working on to make sure I presented her point of view accurately. She was appalled at how many times she used the words 'like' and 'right?' superfluously. She asked me to remove them, and I honored her wishes—while the words helped the reader get a sense of this woman, removing them did not change the meaning of what she said.

On the other hand, direct quotes from our participants develop them as characters in our stories. Readers gain a sense of who the participants are, of their voices, which should be different from ours. The words "um" and "like" and "right?" are often placeholders, used when a person is thinking through their words. They may be accompanied with hand gestures, pauses, or other nonverbal communication that is just as important as their verbalizations.

Here's an example of a quote with those placeholders and without. I asked my son to tell me about his school. In the first example, I include his nonverbal cues and verbal pauses. I edit them out in the second. Do the two quotes read differently? Does the removal of the placeholders seem to change the meaning of the quote?

Me: Tell me something about your school.

Unedited response: Um, we do, we learn, um, [computer] programming, um, we, uh, do all sorts of…all-school activities. Um. [pause] We have nice teachers. [pause, finger popping] We…get to go to the park a lot. And, lastly…we…learn lots of advanced math?

Edited response: We learn [computer] programming. We do all sorts of all-school activities. We have nice teachers. We get to go to the park a lot. And lastly, we learn lots of advanced math.

We also need to be cognizant of the ethical implications here. How we portray our participants speaks to the authenticity of our representation. Hart (2011: 86) notes that "the reluctance to present people as they really speak is, I suppose, understandable. If you quote an uneducated hayseed verbatim, you may look like an arrogant city swell. But isn't it always arrogant to substitute your own manner of speaking for someone else's, as though yours were the only English acceptable in polite company? And isn't the rich patios of an authentic American dialect more likely to convey the color of daily life, the variety of our culture or honest emotion?"

Write It Up

1. Choose three quotes from your own research. Write each verbatim and then write it again, this time editing out extraneous words and subverbalizations. Does editing the quote change your perspective on what the participant said?

FIRST, SECOND, OR THIRD PERSON

Ethnography is conventionally written in first person, from the researcher's point of view. Point of view is analogous to the camera angle in film—we see the action through a particular perspective. In this case we see the action from the perspective of the researcher. As Saldaña (2011) notes, writing in first person is more personable that writing in third. Using first person we can connect directly with the reader.

One consideration you must address when writing in first person is how present the researcher 'I' is in your narrative. Ask yourself, whose story is this? Yours or the participants? Too much researcher 'I' and the reader may perceive your narrative as narcissistic and accuse you of the dreaded 'navel gazing.' If passages seem too much about you and not enough about the event you're discussing, zoom out your camera, use a wider angle and provide more description outside of you. While the writing is in first person, it can still be about something other than yourself. Of course if the story is about you, such as in autoethnography, your camera angle will be much narrower. If autoethnography is not your goal, however, you can still tell the story in first person without *becoming* the story (Hart, 2011).

Second person writing is generally reserved for guidebooks and instruction manuals (like this one). While it is possible to write a research report in second person, you are ill advised to do so, as even experienced writers find that writing ethnography in second person is difficult to do well. When we write in second person, we assume a high level of familiarity with the reader. This works in instructional writing because you know that your reader came to your work with a particular goal—to learn from you. The writing can be personable and intimate. This technique is more difficult to pull off when there is more distance between you and your reader.

A third person narrator is omnipotent, able to see outside of the characters' heads to a wider perspective. Writing in third person captures external reality. I sometimes use third person to describe scenes that I've witnessed. In the passage below, I write about an act of performative environmentalism (Gullion, 2015) that I witnessed in the course of my own ethnographic research in third person (I corroborated the text of Death's speech with a website that posted it after her talk):

A young woman approaches the lectern. She is dressed in black, her face painted the white of a skull, with darkened, hollowed eyes and lips. She leans in to the microphone.

"Hello everyone. I am Death and I'm here to thank you."

A man on the dais interrupts her to ask "Will you please state your name and address for the record?"

The woman complies, but with the interruption Death has lost some of her charisma.

"So, as I said, I am Death and I'm here to thank you," she continues.

First of all, thank you for not taking the safety of our community seriously. Thank you for appointing several individuals…that are associated with natural gas companies on our task force. Companies that consistently distort the truth. Thank you for allowing less than 1,000 feet between our homes and frack wells. Wells that could easily explode. Thank you for not establishing a methane monitoring program. Thank you for putting very few safeguards to protect surrounding communities from accidents and leaks. Thank you for basically ignoring the harmful air emissions that pollute communities surrounding drilling operations, compressor stations and pipelines. Thank you for allowing water contamination from substandard drill casings. Thank you for making only a few of your meetings public. So, that residents of [your] community have hardly any input on issues concerning the safety of their city. Thank you for ignoring the negative health effects associated with natural gas drilling. Thank you for allowing a corporation to bully our community. Thank you for ignoring climate change. The pollution associated with fracking, such as carbon dioxide, accelerates the effects of climate change. And one last thing, thank you for making my job, as Death, easy (We Are Power Shift, 2012)

During the young woman's talk, the men on the dais squirm; the one woman is attentive. One man scribbles on a paper in front of him, the task appearing to consume all his attention. Another gives the audience a bored blank stare. None of them seem frightened of Death's wrath.

Death gathers the pages of her speech and sits back down. The committee moves on.

I wrote this passage in third person in order to portray the depersonalization of the interaction between Death and the city officials listening to her talk. In this case, the third person perspective is a literary device that conveys the mood of the scene.

The danger of writing in third person though is that you can create too much distance between yourself and your reader. Most 'scientific' writing is written in third person, with an omnipotent narrator, mimicking the so-called ideal of objectivity. Yet this voice often writes around the topic, muddying and detracting from the work itself (Saldaña, 2011). Writing in first person allows the reader to connect with you as the writer, to have the sort of hermeneutic exchange that exemplifies good academic work. Writing in first person also assigns responsibility for the ideas presented in the text: I wrote this, these are my ideas. Not the papers'. Mine. 'This paper' does not show anything. I do. And for goodness sake, don't refer to yourself as 'the author.' How pedantic. This author is telling you, don't do it.

You may find that you shift perspective in a single piece (like I have done in this section) and that is okay. Different scenes may call for different points of view. Just make sure that you don't make your reader dizzy with a lot of perspective changes—the reader should not have to work to figure out what is going on. Just like a bored reader, a frustrated reader won't be your reader for long.

Write It Up

1. Write a passage from your own research in first, second, and third person. Which perspective works best for that passage?

ACTIVE/PASSIVE

Brenda Phillips, a prolific disaster researcher and exceptional scholar, is one of my mentors. And she would hate that sentence. Not because I praise her (although she is humble), but because of my use of passive voice. Back in graduate school, when I gave her papers to read, she circled 'is,' 'was,' and 'to be' and all the other generic words I used and handed it back to me, ACTIVE VOICE written in big letters across the top of the first page. She forced me not only to improve my writing, but to stake a claim in the marketplace of ideas.

"Active voice," Hart (2011: 115) writes, "advances the narrative by showing why and how human beings affect the world around them." Consider who does the action in your sentences, along with what action you want to portray. Remember way back in about junior high when you learned to diagram sentences? That skill will come in handy in your writing today. But you don't need to draw out the entire diagram (you can if you want to). All you need to look at for now is the subject of the sentence and the verb.

I hate reading articles that begin like this: "This paper explores teacher-student communication and suggests several techniques teachers can employ inside and outside of the classroom."

No. This paper does not do these things. The author does. This is better: "In this paper, I explore teacher-student communication and suggest several techniques teachers can employ inside and outside of the classroom."

In this case, the author is the actor, not the piece of paper. Not only does assigning 'this paper' authority place the author in a passive position, but it also weakens the author's overall argument. Take responsibility (and pride) in the work and claim it. Plant your flag in the sand.

Passive voice excludes significant information. Becker (1986: 74) also argues that one way to cut much of the passive voice in your work is by identifying the actor: "We seldom think that things just happen by themselves, as passive verbs suggest, because in our daily lives people do things and make them happen. Sentences that name active agents make our representations of social life more understandable and believable." Who is doing the thing? Passive writing takes the authority and responsibility away from the researcher.

Passive voice may also muddy your theoretical argument. Becker (1986: 8) wrote, "If you say, for example, that 'deviants were labeled,' you don't have to say who labeled them. That is a theoretical error, not just bad writing." Because one of the key points of labeling theory involves the relative power positions among the labeled and the labeler. The deviants were not labeled out of thin air. Perhaps their teachers labeled them deviant. That would be more in keeping with labeling theory.

Now that we are paying attention to who is doing the action, let's look at the action they are taking with this passage:

> Brenda is an animal rescuer. She has a toy poodle from a puppy mill raid.

While both of these sentences are true, we can strengthen them by replacing "is" and "has" with action verbs:

> Brenda *rescues* animals. She *saved* her toy poodle from a puppy mill.

Brenda is not a passive animal lover. She rescues and saves them! See how much stronger we made that assertion? Ascribe intent and embrace action verbs.

Of course, sometimes passive voice is appropriate—when we want to represent something as fixed or static, passive voice helps portray that feeling. Here is an example of how to use passive voice in that way:

> Stephanie and I can spend hours in a coffee shop talking about research. When she tells me stories about Goddesses (her current research obsession), she illustrates with grand hand gestures. She once knocked a glass of water in her lap while telling me a story about the Hindu Goddess Sitala. She shrieked and laughed and pulled a handful of napkins from the dispenser on the table to mop up the mess.

> At work, Stephanie is reserved. She is worried that her colleagues won't respect her research. She tucks her Goddess woman necklace into her purse when she is on campus. When she talks about her work at all, she discusses methodology in general terms.

Notice the transition from active to passive voice in this passage. In the first paragraph, I use active voice (she tells, illustrates, knocked, shrieked, laughed, pulled) to demonstrate how dynamic Stephanie is one-on-one. The first sentence of the next paragraph employs a more passive voice—she is reserved. By shifting the movement to a passive stance, we begin to get a sense of the oppression Stephanie probably feels when she believes her work is not respected by her colleagues.

Action verbs allow us to create a sense of movement. They make our work more interesting. One of my graduate students posted a video of himself reading a passage from a textbook I'd assigned for one of my classes out loud on Facebook (as an aside, this is a good reminder to remember who your Facebook friends are when you post stuff). The author wrote the book using a passive voice throughout the whole thing. I felt bad for the students and bad for the author of the text: the book was godawful boring. While it contained a wealth of information about what I believe can be a fascinating topic (sociological aspects of infectious disease transmission), the writing dragged on and on. As he read, my student's normally animated voice slowed and slurred, too dull to make any of the reading interesting, too bored to even continue with the entertainingly mocking performance. His body even began to sag as he read; by the end I thought he would collapse on the floor.

How many months—how many years—did that author work on that book? Presumably, this was that author's *life work*, and my student videotaped himself mocking it on Facebook. You do not want your own work mocked on Facebook. That's a terrible ending to your ethnography. By the end of that particular unit in my course, I had little faith that any of the students read the book in its entirety. Honestly, I skimmed through it myself, and I won't be using that one in future courses.

Don't bore your readers.

Besides, who wants to work that hard on something that people won't read anyway?

Write It Up

1. Read through your manuscript and circle every instance of 'is' or 'to be' or any derivatives thereof. Rewrite those sentences with action verbs.
2. As you edit your sentences, make sure that the reader can clearly identify who is doing the action.

CHAPTER 17

ADVERBS

Every writing manual says get rid of all your adverbs.

Like using passive voice, adverbs signal a greater need to find an action verb. For example, rather than writing that the girl slowly walked along the path, let's think of an action verb to describe her pace. Is she meandering? Sauntering? Snaking? Rambling? Moseying? Ambling?

As Ariel Gore (2007: 84) writes, "You didn't become a writer because you wanted to tell me that your brother 'retorted angrily.' You became a writer because you needed to show me the veins bulging from his neck, or how the wood of the door frame felt against your skull the night you went crazy. Tell me *that* story."

When editing your manuscript, identify all the adverbs you use. Try to replace them with actions verbs. Maybe you can't *quite* cut all of them. That's ok. But try.

Write It Up

1. Read through a passage that you've written from your own research. Identify all adverbs. Rewrite those sentences, using adjectives and action verbs to replace the adverbs.

SHOW, DON'T TELL

You've probably heard the maxim, show, don't tell. In telling, it is easier for your critics to pelt you with accusations of bias, particularly when your colorful adjectives read like your personal opinion rather than based in your research. For example, I can write, "The conditions at the county jail are deplorable." That sounds like my opinion, like I personally believe the conditions at the jail are deplorable, but that an objective observer might not draw the same conclusion. And while it may in fact be my opinion, my argument becomes much stronger when I *show* you the deplorable conditions at the county jail, when I give you enough information to enable you to reach my conclusion on your own:

> Joan wakes with a start—someone is pulling her hair. She reaches through the darkness to find a warm furry mass. She leaps from her bunk, squealing, disgusted. It's the third night in a row she's woken to rats chewing on her hair. Her bunkmates scream at her: 'Shut the fuck up, bitch!' She lays back down on the concrete platform, puts her arm under her head as a pillow, and cries.

The details of Joan's story are gathered from interview transcripts and observations conducted at the jail. I put them into a narrative form to tell the story of the deplorable conditions at the jail. Readers do not have to rely on me to tell them that the conditions are deplorable—they can see that for themselves. Rats chewing your hair? Concrete bunks with no pillow? People cursing at you? Yeah, that sounds pretty deplorable to me. There are additional details that the writer could include to further round out the story. The room smells like sewage because the toilets back up nearly every day. A glob of rotten milk goes in Joan's mouth when she takes a sip from her carton. Show the reader this slice of the social world. Lead them through your theoretical argument with your words. Give them pieces of information to help them draw the conclusions you found.

Greetz (1973) invites ethnographers to engage in thick description. Through the use of thick description, the researcher not only shows the reader a scenario from the research, but also provides a depth of support for the researcher's analytical argument through the inclusion of copious details.

Let's look at another example of how to do this. Suppose during the course of an in-depth interview with a retired army veteran, a researcher learns that to help with the transition to retirement, one of the veterans in the study joined a peer-counseling project to help combat soldiers re-acclimate to their lives in the US. The researcher could legitimately represent this idea with the following statement:

> I didn't know what to do with my free time. I joined the peer-counseling program, and I felt a sense of purpose, like I could really contribute.
> – Female respondent, age 66

This is a fine quote and gives the reader some good information. In a brief write up of the study, this would be adequate. But let's look at the same statement embedded in thick description. Drawing from the researcher's field notes, the researcher can sketch a scene that will give much more insight into the participant's story, shifting the perspective from *respondent* to *person*, humanizing and contextualizing the events:

> Barbara's salt and pepper hair is pulled up into a bun. She sets a plate of steaming scones on the kitchen table between us. She insists I take one to eat with the coffee with condensed milk she made me. She tells me the condensed milk is a habit she picked up in the Army. "I didn't know what to do with all my free time," she said when I asked her about retirement. "I joined the peer counseling program, and I felt a sense of purpose, like I could really contribute." Her face lights up as she tells me this.

This vignette is not terribly long, yet in telling a story rather than simply including a quote, the respondent is personified. She has a name—Barbara. While a pseudonym to protect her privacy, naming her rather than referring to her as 'female' begins to give her a personality. We know she is retired— that is the topic of the study and is reaffirmed when the researcher asked her about retirement. We also know Barbara has salt and pepper hair. If her exact age, 66, is not relevant, these two bits of information are likely enough to give the reader a sense of her age. The scones steam, suggesting either that she made them from scratch or that she's reheated them. She insists the researcher eat one. She's also made the researcher coffee, but not just any coffee, coffee with condensed milk, a habit she picked up in the Army, one that isn't typical in most of America. The drink is something special to her, made by her to share with the researcher. The offering of scones and the coffee are caretaking gestures. They give us additional clues about this person. Barbara has gone out of her way to take care of the researcher, and she is meeting with the researcher in her home. This aspect of her personality comes through in the interview—as a peer counselor, she also takes care of people. The story tells us that caretaking brings her gratification—her face lights up as she talks about her work—which lends emphasis to her statement about finding a purpose through participation in the peer counseling program.

Thick description invites readers into the world of your ethnography, and compelling details draw the reader into your story. Think about what details caught your eye during your fieldwork. Your field notes are probably filled with compelling details. Show those details to your reader. If something caught your eye it will likely be of interest to them. Compelling details bring context to your work, and help to immerse your reader in the world of your ethnography.

Using our thick description, we contextualize our ethnography for our readers. To do this, think about and insert sensual details. Tell us what different aspects of your field looked like, and also include other sensory details.

Describe the smells you encountered. Did the room smell of stale beer? Or gardenias? Maybe the clinic waiting room smelled like bleach, with an undertone of body odor. Or the alley behind the tire shop where you talked with the gang member smelled so strongly of rubber and diesel exhaust, it made your head swim.

How did it sound? Did the trucks along the highway drone out the chants of the protestors? Was the music at the nightclub so loud that you had to rely on lip reading to understand anyone's words? Or was the waiting room unnaturally quite, as everyone looked at their smart phones, and no one spoke to each other?

How did the spaces you entered feel? Was it so hot that beads of sweat ran down your back? Were the plastic chairs uncomfortable? Were they broken, so that when you sat down the back of the chair wobbled and you nearly fell on the floor? Was the room so crowded you felt claustrophobic? Did the stabbing of the tattoo needle bring tears to your eyes?

Evoke sensual, visceral details—put the reader in that place. Narayan (2012: 36) suggests that we "describe the emotional and bodily sensations of moving through a place." Describe the spaces, rhythms, sounds, scents. Describe the general. Describe the specific. Describe objects. Describe the hidden places. What did you see or experience that others might not? Sketch the margins, illuminate the shadows.

CHAPTER 18

High quality ethnographic data is the foundation of your story. Draw on your field notes, memos, and other data for those sensual and textual details. "Good writing springs from good data," Madden (2010: 152) writes. "Evocation, thick description, persuasion, and a nice turn of phrase are so much easier to accomplish when you've got the data organized and marshaled behind you." Show us your world in your writing.

Those descriptions are vital, they give your ethnography life. Be cognizant of how you use them. Along with thick description and character development, remember to consider the pacing of your text like we talked about earlier when we looked at story arcs. Remember to use action verbs in your thick description.

Write It Up

1. List five compelling details from your field notes. Use them to describe a scene from your field to someone who has never been in that setting. Include sensual descriptions, such as how the place looked, sounded, smelled, and felt.
2. Create a composite character—a person who exemplifies the people in your research. Write a character sketch. Explain who this person is, give them a name, descriptive characteristics, and a background story.

CONVERSATIONS

People have conversations, and including conversations in your writing gives the reader additional clues about the people and events in your story. "If you want to tell a true story," Hart (2011: 129) writes, "your readers should hear your characters talk to one another." Quotes from the field "lend authority, tell us what others think, and add colorful voices" to the tale (Hart, 2011: 128). There are many ways you can include your participants' words in your ethnography. Let's look at several together. In this example, I use one interview transcript and present it in different ways.

This is an interview I conducted with a woman I've given the pseudonym of Mallory. I will begin with a simple summary of the transcript. It goes like this:

> Mallory said she first learned that natural gas wells would be drilled on her property from her neighbor. She felt like the drillers did not care about her wellbeing at all.

In that passage, I paraphrased Mallory's words from the transcript. Another way to write this up, is to use an extended quote from the transcript:

> They came onto our neighbor's property on August 29, 2009, and that was a Saturday. And I was actually in the living room, working out on my elliptical. And I saw trucks starting to show up, and I thought, that's odd. And a few minutes later my neighbor called me and he said they're coming to put in a well, and there's nothing I can do about it.

This quote gives us more detail and lets the reader listen to Mallory's voice as she tells her own story. Now let's write a conversation. In the interview, Mallory relates a conversation that her neighbor had with representatives from the drilling company. This passage is still a direct quote from the interview transcript. Mallory described the conversation between the neighbor and a man from the natural gas drilling company during her interview:

> My neighbor walked up to the men parked by his pond. "Do you want to fish?" he asked. Because a lot of people come out here to fish, it's

kind of a neighborly thing to let people fish your pond. A man got out of one of the trucks, looking apologetic.

"I'm really sorry," the man said, "but I'm actually looking to see where I'm going to put my bulldozer."

"What bulldozer?" my neighbor asked.

"I'm sorry, we're…they're getting ready to put a gas well here."

We could also embed that conversation into a larger conversation between Mallory and the interviewer, again, relying on the interview transcript for the exact wording of that conversation:

Mallory recounts the conversation with from her neighbor. "He walked up to the men parked by his pond. 'Do you want to fish?' he asked. Because a lot of people come out here to fish, it's kind of a neighborly thing to let people fish your pond. A man got out of one of the trucks, looking apologetic. 'I'm really sorry,' the man said, 'but I'm actually looking to see where I'm going to put my bulldozer.' 'What bulldozer?' my neighbor asked. 'I'm sorry, we're…they're getting ready to put a gas well here.'"

"So it's on his property? Someone just shows up on his property?" I ask.

Mallory nods. "It's like we're not even here."

Each of the above examples remain true to the transcribed conversation between Mallory and the interviewer; the examples are simply presented differently. All of them convey that same feeling as in the original summary: Mallory said she first learned that natural gas wells would be drilled on her property from her neighbor. She felt like the drillers did not care about her wellbeing at all. Our own creativity comes into the writing as we decide how to best present the information. If we wanted to play with the form a bit more, we could also write this scene as an ethnodrama:

Neighbor: Do you want to fish? A lot of people come out here to fish.

Gas Driller: I'm really sorry, but I'm actually looking to see where I'm going to put my bulldozer.

Neighbor: What bulldozer?

Gas Driller: I'm sorry, we're…they're getting ready to put a gas well here.

Or how about a poem?
  Standing by the pond,
  He asked the strangers
  Did they want to fish? No.
  We're looking for a place
  To put the bulldozer.
  It's like we're not even here.

As you can see, we can choose many different ways to present the same information. With these more experimental forms, we can play with the dialog. As you can see, each form continues to maintain the original sense that the drillers are unconcerned with the residents' feeling about their wellbeing. You may want to play with several different lengths and forms to find which works best with the goals of your narrative. In keeping with the ethical concerns we discussed earlier, be sure you alert your reader to what you are doing.

Write It Up

1. Identify a conversation in your own field notes or transcripts that provides compelling evidence for one of your analytic points. Write out that conversation and link it directly to that point.
2. Write a conversation in multiple formats. Which works best to both illustrate your point and draw your reader into your world?

CHARACTERS

I've mentioned characters a number of times, so let's spend some time exploring how to write compelling characters.

We tend to think of characters as people in fictional worlds, but in the case of writing ethnography, we can think of characters as the people you interacted with in the course of your research. They are the people you observed, the people who participated in your ethnography.

Your characters can stand out as unique individuals, or they can represent a class of people. Often in social science research people are divided into categories, or types. To represent these types, you can create what are known as composite characters. These are fictionalized individuals whose characteristics are grounded in your research, who represent a typical case, or group of people. As before, you have an obligation to alert your reader when a person in your narrative is a composite character.

Composite characters can function to explain details of the particular categories in your research, however, we must also be wary of creating flat, stereotypical characters. People are multidimensional. The hero, to be believable, is also flawed. The villain has some likable qualities. These variations add legitimacy to your story because they read as true. We know that people have layers of complexity, and our readers appreciate that the story is not black and white.

For a fantastic example of character development, look at the series *Game of Thrones*. Author George R. R. Martin gives us a wonderful array of complex characters in his tale. I have a love-hate relationship with most the population of his world. They are, from scene-to-scene, alternatively loveable, wicked, virtuous, devious, innocent, and deranged. They are, in a word, human. While your characters might not be plotting to take over the kingdom and sit on the Iron Throne, their humanity should nonetheless shine through your story.

"Character," Hart (2011: 76) writes, "is the key to reader interest. Ultimately, we define ourselves in terms of others. What we really want to know is what, how, and why human beings *do*." And who better to explain those doings than an ethnographer?

It's time for an example. Let's begin by introducing a character from some hypothetical research:

Patti sells essential oils (EO) through a multi-level marketing company. Like many EO Reps, as they're called, she's a middle class stay-at-home mom who not only uses essential oils herself, but also sells them to earn extra money. While she adores staying home and raising her children, she feels a bit guilty that she is not working for pay. Her EO income, while small, alleviates that feeling.

So far in this story, Patti is a composite character. She is a fiction, there is no 'Patti,' but she is also an example of the typical case, based in research. Her status as a stay-at-home mom who uses EO sales to supplement the family income is similar to most of the people in the research project. Now let's add an anecdote specific to Patti to both personify her and to give the reader some insight into this world. This anecdote comes from one of the transcripts. While the details might be different, this story is very similar to others heard throughout the research. We can use this story as belonging to our composite character:

Since childhood, Patti suffered with skin problems. She always thought she'd grow out of them, but then learned about the dreaded adult-acne. It seems like a small thing: I have bad skin. But it wasn't, not to her.

Patti didn't have blemishes. She had severe cystic acne that left her skin hollowed out like the face of the moon. In high school the kids called her Golf Ball. She'd been to doctors and dermatologists. Been on birth control pills and Accutane. Those helped, but she had to quit them to have kids and the acne came back. Benzoyl peroxide only made her skin worse, inflaming her pimples and drying out the surrounding skin until it flaked off.

Her friend Sheila gave her a finger-sized glass roller bottle decorated with blue and purple washi tape. The bottle held a mixture of Vitamin E oil and an essential oil blend.

"I can't put that on my skin," Patti told her. "My skin is already too oily."

"Just try it," Sheila told her. "Every night before bed. Just try."

Patti tried the concoction, and within just a few days her inflammation and redness notably calmed. After two weeks of use her skin looked better then she could ever remember. The oily sheen that she blotted with tissue papers throughout the day disappeared. And for the first time since elementary school, Patti left the house without makeup.

"It was a miracle. I was hooked," Patti said.

Patti has lined the medicine cabinet in her bathroom with small bottles of essential oils. She earns some money from selling the oils, so she feels like she is contributing to the household income, albeit a small amount. And she uses her oils for all sorts of minor ailments. But her motivation is sharing them. "I love my oils," she says. "I want to help other people heal themselves, like Sheila helped me."

Patti is a good example of an average participant in this study. The anecdote, drawn from interview transcripts, personifies her. The reader can feel her story, can imagine how life-changing this event was for her, and can begin to better understand this group of people. This is what we want our ethnography to do. Not every person in this study has the same story as Patti, but they have stories that are similar—they had some illness that essential oils made better. Patti is an example of the type of story one would find in this group of women, and this, of course, should be explained to the reader in the narrative and the analysis.

Descriptive details help the reader imagine your characters. We don't need pages of them; as I've mentioned before, just a few details will tap into your reader's knowledge base and create an image for them. For example, if I write that Jason is a tall, thin man with a comb-over, you can probably picture Jason in your head. You have preexisting frames of reference that allow you to imagine a tall, thin man with a comb-over. The picture of Jason you hold in your head will probably differ from the picture of Jason that I hold in my head, but that's ok. Clues about people allow for imaginative interaction between reader and text.

Narayarn (2012: 48) suggests that we "evoke the distinctive quirkiness of individuals." Think of the details that make the individuals in your story distinct and use those details in your writing. There are also times when you might want to describe a group of people, to zoom out and give a broader overview. Who are these people?

How did the people you interacted with speak? Did they have a particular intonation to their words? Did they use slang terms? How do they carry their body? How did they stand? Tall or hunched over? Did their bodies take up all the space in the room, or did they fold in on themselves? Did they have any unusual mannerisms? How did they behave one on one? How did they behave in a room full of strangers?

We can provide our readers with all sorts of clues about the people in our ethnography. Details can place a person—for example, if a character is holding a textbook, we can infer that they are a student or academic or scholar. We can give other clues to allow for inferences about gender, age, race, and so forth. For example, details about clothing can tell us something about geographic location and social class. How did they dress? Were they in cowboy boots and jeans? Shorts and tee shirts? Power suits? Or maybe lab coats and scrubs? Did their clothes look like they were purchased at Nordstroms or Walmart?

Anecdotes can help to personify the people in our research. Stories that clue us into the characters' past and motivations not only help to humanize our characters, but also help the reader emotionally identify with them.

Remember as well to parcel out these details over the course of the story. Like George R.R. Martin's characters, people evolve and change over the course of time. Show us that evolution.

Write It Up

1. List 5 characteristics that are general to a group of people in your research. Write a composite character that includes each of those characteristics.
2. Write the background story of one of the actual people in your research. Clue the reader into that person's motivations for action.

METAPHORICALLY SPEAKING

So far, we've talked about narrative structures and story arcs. We've reviewed issues of voice, action, and details. We've looked at how to personify our characters, how to bring them to life on the page. Now let's turn our attention to some of the details that help to raise your writing to an even higher caliber. We'll start with a discussion of integrating metaphors into your work.

Metaphors are analogies that connect two things that seem on the surface to be unrelated, but when pointed out make rhetorical sense. The bruised clouds threatened to rain. My home is in her arms. Metaphors add color to our stories, and help us to continue to tap into the reader's imagination. We can use metaphors as touchstones within the story itself, or, even better, we can highlight the metaphors that our participants use as a literary device in our writing. "Ethnographers can gain descriptive depth by being alert not just to metaphors that enliven their own perception," Narayan (2012: 33) writes, "but also to the metaphors that people living in a place regularly use."

What metaphors do the participants in your ethnography use? Do the tornado victims describe the remnants of their neighborhood as a war zone? Do people in the community describe the Ebola outbreak as a zombie apocalypse?

One way to approach both your writing and analysis is to present and unpack the meanings behind the metaphors your participants use. Metaphors often represent much more than one would assume from the initial statement. As I worked on my natural gas drilling ethnography, the participants repeatedly used rape metaphors to describe their experiences. They spoke of the rape of the land by fracking, and they said they felt sexually violated by the gas companies. I *hated* this metaphor. I was very resistant to using it. In my mind, nothing is like rape but rape, and I never want to diminish the experiences of a rape survivor by comparing that experience to something that is not rape. This was clearly a bias that I brought to the research, and I needed to engage in a lot of personal reflexive practice to understand and overcome it. Because despite my misgivings, the participants in my study kept alluding to the metaphor, to such an extent that not to discuss it would be disingenuous. I had to address the metaphor in order to provide an authentic representation of their experience.

Through reflexive and analytic work, I unpacked the meanings of that metaphor, both for myself and for the participants. I came to realize that the people in the research didn't have the language—the words simply didn't exist—to describe how violated they felt. The closest they could come to expressing that violation was to compare it to a rape. This spoke to a real need for environmental justice as well as a discussion of sexual environmental violence that I may not have seen if it were not for the metaphor. Ultimately, the metaphor gave me tools to engage deeper in my analytic work, to capture a facet of what was happening in the field that I might have otherwise missed.

I still don't like the metaphor. But I don't have to.

Metaphors add color and depth to your work. There is one caveat, however, that you need to keep in mind when using metaphors in your writing. "To make sense to the reader," LeCompte and Schensul (2013: 282) write, "the item that is being used metaphorically must be familiar to the audience whom the ethnographer wants to reach." Saying something is like running a horse through barrels may be meaningful to people familiar with the rodeo, but have little meaning to people without that point of reference. Make sure—to the best of your ability—your intended audience will understand your references.

Write It Up

1. Identify one metaphor that your participants use. What does that metaphor mean to them? How might you incorporate it in your writing?
2. Write a short scene from your research. Use a metaphor creatively in that scene.

VIGNETTES

LeCompte and Schensul (2013: 269) define vignettes as "snapshots or short descriptions of events or people that evoke the overall picture the ethnographer is trying to paint." These brief, often dramatic scenes lack the full development of a story arc, but nonetheless offer some truth up to the reader.

I often use vignettes to begin new sections in my writing. I start with a vignette and transition into exposition and/or analysis. In this example from my book, *Fracking the Neighborhood* (2015), I begin a chapter on the perceived health effects of natural gas development with a vignette crafted from an interview transcript:

Ahmed is afraid of storms. He's afraid of what happens at a natural gas pad site when a storm knocks out the power.

"I was literally gassed in my own home in the middle of the night," he tells me. "It sounds very sensationalized. We lost power because of a wicked storm that blew through. We heard an explosion that was like a transformer that must have blown. It threw the compressor station offline. Pressure built up in the system here. I had opened the windows after the storm passed and a cool front had blown in. I like the fresh air. And then we heard this. Venting like this." He makes a sound: "ZHHHZHHHZHHH."

Really loud. It jolted us up. I heard this noise and I started to shake. I was terrified. I thought, oh my gosh, what is happening? I knew it was off the [gas] site because I could hear what direction it was coming from. So then I called 911.

My house filled with gas or something. I don't even know what it was, but it stunk. It smelled dirty. It smelled like...like the inside of a bicycle tube tire. Maybe kind of what that would smell like. It was very strong and it rushed into my house because the winds were whipping from all directions that night.

Ahmed's concerns were supported by both a Texas Commission on Environmental Quality (TCEQ) report that the gas well by his home vented due to increases in pressure and by emails from the company who owns the well. Both reported the event as small, with low amounts of gas released. Ahmed believes that the release was much bigger than records from that night indicate.

"They've got to burp that stuff out or it will explode. It covered the neighborhood like a heavy, it had a heavy feel, and I'm feeling like a crazy person because everyone is telling me nothing is lighter than air and it just dissipates and it's odorless. Well, what was this?" he asked. "This was something else. I still, to this day, do not know what we were exposed to. And I'm looking at my eleven-year-old daughter lying in bed, innocently sleeping, and I'm thinking, 'Oh my gosh, she's getting gassed in her sleep. She's getting a chemical exposure.' So we're quickly shutting the windows, but it was too late. All the gunk was already in there and you couldn't go outside."

Vignettes help set up a scene for your reader. After this vignette, I go into technical detail about the scientific studies on the toxins associated with natural gas drilling sites. While a brief, stand-alone scene, the vignette sets up a question in the readers mind: What *is* being released at these gas sites? I then lead the reader through a discussion of the possibilities. The technical details of chemical compounds and health effects are framed with a story of a real family, a real little girl, who was "gassed in her sleep." The vignette stands alone—there is no further development of this particular narrative. We don't learn what, if anything, happened to Ahmed and his daughter after this incidence. It is a literary device whose purpose is to place the question in the reader's mind and to set an emotional tone over the material that is to come.

Write It Up

1. Write a vignette to frame a section of your analytic writing.

ON SOUNDING SMART

Many academics hold an incorrect assumption that using big words and convoluted prose makes them sound smarter (Becker, 1986). Becker (1986) quotes one of his students on this. She said, "The way someone writes—the more difficult the writing style—the more intellectual they sound." This thinking is common in academia. We think to ourselves, "I'm a smart person and if I don't understand someone's big words, well, they must be *really* smart."

Many of us are guilty of using jargon as an elite membership card. With some of my peers, I can talk about "speculative realism," and "rhizomes," and "assemblages," and they will have a shared understanding of those terms. But I also know that I can throw those words around in a different group and my language will be inaccessible. While some of my audience may assume I'm being a pompous ass, some of them will think that I must be really smart.

C. Wright Mills (1959: 218–219, as quoted in Becker 1986: 31) writes that the "lack of ready intelligibility [in scholarly writing], I believe, usually has little or nothing to do with the complexity of the subject matter, and nothing at all to do with the profundity of thought. It has to do almost entirely with certain confusions of the academic writer about his [sic] own status....To overcome the academic *prose* you have to overcome the academic *post*."

Yes, we want people to think we're smart. We're intellectuals after all. We want our work to be respected intellectual discourse. But we don't want to write "polysyllabic bullshit" (Becker, 1986) either.

Saldaña (2011: 141) advocates for elegance in writing. "Elegance means *simplicity*. Writing that is elegant relies on trusting the power of the research tale itself; told in a clear and straightforward manner. You needn't try to impress anyone with convoluted prose. It is most often the *ideas* that will make a lasting impact and impression on your reader," he writes.

Think about what you are trying to say, the ideas that you want your work to convey. What argument are you making? What ideas are you putting forth, and how are you translating those ideas for your reader? Can your reader understand your argument?

Stephen King (2000: 110), who knows a thing or two about writing successful narratives, offers the following advice:

One of the really bad things you can do to your writing is to dress up the vocabulary, looking for long words because you're maybe a bit ashamed of your short ones. This is like dressing up a household pet in evening clothes. The pet is embarrassed and the person who committed this act of premeditated cuteness should be even more embarrassed. Make yourself a solemn promise right now that you'll never use 'emolument' when you mean 'tip' and you'll never say John stopped long enough to perform an act of excretion when you mean John stopped long enough to take a shit....I'm not trying to get you to talk dirty, only plain and direct. Remember the basic rule of vocabulary is *use the first word that comes to your mind, if it is appropriate and colorful."*

You may be thinking, yeah, but that's Stephen King. He writes fiction. His work isn't scholarly. Ok, that's true. But the point remains: You want someone to read your work and being pedantic isn't going to draw them in. I can't tell you how many papers I've read by students who obfuscate their own points cashing in on ten-letter words trying to sound smart. It doesn't make me like them; I just find it annoying.

Take a look around your own workspace. How many of those books and articles did you only partly read? What made you stop reading or skip through large chunks of text? Was any of the writing inaccessible?

This is not to say that we can never use big words. You can use big words if you want to. Just don't bullshit your reader with them. Don't use big words to try to make yourself sound smarter. Because in the end you won't come across that way, and your book with gather dust on someone's shelf.

Write It Up

1. Review a passage that you have written for one of these Write It Up prompts (you *are* doing these, right?). Replace or define any jargon for your reader.

CHAPTER 24

EDITING

Thanks to the genius of cut and paste, writing need not be linear. I wrote this book by hand in a small lined notebook with a bird on the cover. I carted it around in my purse so I could jot down my thoughts as they occurred to me. I wrote the first few sections in a small cabin in Oklahoma. I wrote the chapter on thick description first. I rewrote that last sentence three times. I typed everything from that notebook into one file on my computer. I printed it, double spaced, so I could write by hand all over it, and then I carried that around everywhere I went. I wrote and scratched out and drew all over those pages. I then typed my changes into the computer and began the process again, et cetera, until I felt finished. This strategy may not resonate with you, but it works for me, and that is how I've written everything I've ever published.

Nothing we write comes out perfect with the first draft. That's why we have drafts—we write, rewrite, and edit. Lamott (1994: 22) writes, "For me and most of the other writers I know, writing is not rapturous. In fact, the only way I can get anything written at all is to write really shitty first drafts."

This is why half the task of writing is editing. I realize that as social scientists we are not supposed to overgeneralize, but I'm going to. All writers (all of them, even if they deny it) write shitty first drafts. All writers struggle. We all write awkward sentences and make grammatical blunders. And that's ok. Because half the task of writing is editing.

No one has to see your first draft. Or your second. Until your work is actually published, it can be changed. You can shift, massage, and rewrite your words until they read how you want them to.

Remember earlier when I told you to let your inner editor play with some kittens so you could get some writing done? It's time for her to put those kittens down, to sharpen her pencil, and come back to your project. It's time for her to help you with some serious, hard work.

I find that many students who have writing that has a lot of potential tend to skip through the editing process. Sometimes I hear them in the hallway outside my office before class (or I see their posts on Facebook), and they say that they stayed up late the night before writing their papers. Or worse, that they wrote their papers in the hours before their class meets. I know that they didn't do the work of editing because they didn't give themselves time to do a good job.

I don't want to sound too harsh—maybe they did some basic copy editing and fixed some run-on sentences. But they didn't do the real work of editing, the roll-up-your-sleeves hard work of editing, and that shows in their writing.

A writer must craft their shitty first drafts into something wonderful. And that crafting takes sit-in-your-chair work.

When I feel like I am finished with a piece, I stick it in a drawer (literally or metaphorically) to percolate for a couple of weeks before I go through it for a good edit. Some writers advocate a longer wait (Stephen King suggests six weeks or more). The idea is that you need to be able to look at the manuscript with fresh eyes, to read what is actually written on the page and not what you meant to say. And this is how I know that students who write their papers the night before it is due didn't do the work of editing. They never gave themselves a chance to see their work how it is really written.

Not only will your manuscript benefit from a fresh-eyed reading in entirety, but this part is fun, because when you've stepped away from your writing for a bit and come back to it, you get to see how much potential your piece really has.

I find that I edit better on paper than on a screen. When reading on a monitor, my brain reads what I intended to write, and not always the exact words I wrote. I catch errors more readily on paper. So to begin editing, I print out the document and start to comb through it.

As you edit, you have two jobs, one micro and one macro, and this may take several readings to get through. Your micro job is to catch typos and grammatical errors that you've missed until this point. Think about the mechanics of the work, the sentence structures and the transitions between paragraphs and sections. Look for choppy, undeveloped sentences, or for sentences that run on too long, or that are confusing. Fix your adverb and passive voice problems. Cut any unnecessary words ('as well as' can be written as 'and'). Delete the clutter. Find every instance of "it" or "he" or "she" and make sure you have a clear referent. Will the reader know what "it" is?

Make sure that all of your citations are in your reference section (check vice versa as well) and that all of your references are complete (cheers to you if yours are all good—no matter how hard I try to keep an eye on this, I always have to fix citation problems). Check your work for shift and drift errors—names that change during the course of the piece (I once shifted Johnston to Johnson halfway through an article; in a quite embarrassing turn of events, Dr Johnston was one of the reviewers for the article, and he caught the error). Watch for objects that change also (i.e. your protagonist arrived in a truck and left on a motorcycle).

If your manuscript is too long (and unless you are writing a book, your publishing venue probably has a strict page limit) cut the length. Every word in that piece should be relevant. If it isn't, cut it.

I tend to have the opposite problem in my writing. My early training was as a poet and journalist. Unless I'm writing poetry, my writing tends to be underdeveloped. I try to pack too much meaning in too few words, and I find that I need to add details back in.

I typically advise people to read their work out loud to help with the editing process. This may not be the best option for you, however, if you are not writing in your native language or if your command of the language is not good. In that case, find someone to help you with this.

When reading out loud, listen closely to your words. Are the sentences too long? What about the paragraphs? Are you boring yourself? (Hint: that's a bad sign). Where do you stumble in the prose? Does what you are saying make sense? Portions that are difficult to read out loud should be edited until the piece reads smoothly.

Remember, editing is half the process of writing, and editing takes time. Between you and me, I struggle with editing myself. I always feel like I'm *done* with the piece once I've written it, and going back through the manuscript over and over is so tedious that I have to force myself to do it. I edit on the computer screen, on printed pages of the text, and by reading out loud. I do each because I have found that with each form I see and hear the text differently. I catch different problems. Sometimes when reading in one format, my eye skips over problem areas because I know what it is *supposed* to say and my brain reads the words that way. This is a common issue for people. I can, however, see those mistakes when I process my text in a different format. Likewise, I catch awkward sentence structures by reading them out loud. If I get tongue-tied, I know I need to fix a problem.

You should also keep an eye on the structure of the pages themselves. Break up the paragraphs if they are too long (please don't keep multi-page paragraphs). Make sure you don't have sentences that carry on for more than four lines. Too much text on a page tires your reader's eyes; keep some white space on your pages.

Your macro job is to consider the overall structure, logic, and flow of the piece. Remember our story arc? Map your manuscript to your story arc, checking for transitions, cliff-hangers, and pacing. I write fast and my writing can be fast-paced. I sometimes have to slow the action down and develop scenes when I edit.

Ask yourself, what is this manuscript about? Then read it again. Do you clearly answer that question? By the last sentence, will the reader know what this manuscript was about too? Will the reader come to the same conclusion as you do on that point?

"Every book—at least every one worth reading—is about *something*." King (2000: 201) writes. "Your job during or just after the first draft is to decide what something or somethings yours is about. Your job in the second draft—or one of them, anyway—is to make that something even more clear. This may necessitate some big changes and revisions. The benefits to you and your reader will be clearer focus and a more unified story."

As you read, watch for any gaping holes in the narrative. I find this happens when I expect the reader to read my mind instead of the document. Did you explain all of the concepts you used? Did you logically connect the points of your argument and lead the reader through them? Do you provide enough evidence to make your claims believable? Think about your work from the perspective of your audience and make sure that you've given them enough information to understand your arguments.

Create an outline of your document. Does the order and progression of the piece make logical sense? If not, take advantage of copy and paste and rearrange the sections. As I begin to type words into a document, I create a rough outline. I can then fill in each of the sections in any order I wish. Sometimes I will just insert a section heading as a reminder to develop that part later. Writing for me is a very nonlinear process, therefore it is very important for me to at some point analyze the structure and rearrange as needed. For example, when writing this book, I had information on publishing in the first section, where I wrote about ethnography in general. The more I thought about it, the more sense it made to me to move that section further to the back of the book—it seemed a more logical progression to have a section on editing, then one on naming the piece, and then one on publishing. Thanks to the genius who invented cut and paste, I rearranged the sections quickly.

Once all of the kinks are worked out, show the piece to someone you trust for feedback. If you are a student, ask your major professor or other mentor to read it. If you have a writing group, share it with them. Oftentimes tenured faculty will look at manuscripts for their tenure-track colleagues. A critical eye before submission will improve your chances of publication.

I know that if I ask my husband to read my work, he will rave about how great it is. And I like that, it is really nice to hear and I feel good about myself when he does that. But at this stage in the process, it is important to find someone less worried about making you feel good and more worried about the publishability of the piece. You need an honest critique.

In return, you need to make sure you don't take that critique personally. Critique of your writing has nothing to do with your worth as an individual. The publishing world is not always kind. Take critiques for what they are— suggestions on how to improve *this particular piece of writing*—and don't inflate them to anything else. Be honest with yourself about the feedback and fix what needs to be fixed.

There is one danger you must be cautious of however. And that is finding yourself caught up in a never-ending trap of perfectionism, unable to stop editing your work. This happened to a Master's student of mine who I finally made submit her two-hundred-plus-page thesis. It was wonderful, but she edited the thing to death. She graduated after I told her she was not allowed to edit the thesis any more. Was it perfect? Probably not. I certainly wasn't going to tell her that; she'd already spent months editing the thing. But the best thesis (or dissertation for that matter) is a finished one.

"Perfection is the voice of the oppressor," Lamott (2007: 28) writes, "the enemy of the people. It will keep you cramped and insane your whole life, and it is the main obstacle between you and a shitty first draft." If you are going to be a successful writer (and I have faith that you are) you have to get over any perfectionism. Now.

Write your draft. Edit it. Get some feedback and fix any problems. Then submit it for publication. The piece will more than likely require additional editing, but at this point you should have an editor's (or an advisor's if this is your thesis/dissertation) guidance on what is left to be done.

Write It Up

1. Be honest with yourself: How much time do you spend editing what you write?
2. Print out something that you've written for one of these Write It Up prompts. Put the pages in a drawer. Wait two weeks. Take them back out and read them. Did you see the work any differently?

CHAPTER 25

ARTS-BASED RESEARCH

Maybe your ethnography isn't going to work as a written piece. Maybe this project needs to be danced or painted or acted out. Arts-based research (ABR) is outside the scope of this text, but I wanted to mention it, just in case what I've written here about writing ethnography isn't working for you. There are endless options for how to represent your work—and those representations doesn't have to be textual. ARB taps into alternate ways of knowing that you simply cannot express via the written word. I encourage ethnographers to learn about these methods and consider incorporating them in their own work.

SECTION III

LINGER IN THE SCENE

CHAPTER 26

PUTTING WORDS ON THE PAGE

Carol and I sit at Starbucks, sipping cinnamon chais. She intrigues me with stories from her research on conservative religious couples in BDSM relationships. I flip through the stack of her transcripts and find an eloquent example that illustrates a point she's just made. I interrupt her, tapping on the pile of paper. "What's next?" I ask. "What are you writing?"

She shrugs in frustration. "I haven't written anything," she said. She tells me she feels stuck. With a goldmine of fascinating data, she's overwhelmed and doesn't know where to begin.

"If there is one process that creates mystique, ritual, and anxiety more than any other in ethnography," Madden (2010: 155) writes, "then it is writing." Most qualitative researchers have been in Carol's situation at one point or another due to the sheer volume of data we horde. That beauty of ethnography—the ability to collect in-depth data over time—can also be its curse. Collecting and organizing all of that data is a tremendous undertaking. Qualitative researchers often amass thousands of pages of data. And oftentimes the data are so rich, we wonder how on earth we will do it all justice on the page. How do we move from data collecting to writing?

Ideally, you have been writing *something* all this time, in your field notes and with your memoing. In fact, like Carol, you may be further along than you realize.

The problem was not that Carol didn't have anything to say. The problem was the blank white space of the first page. Many of us experience that problem. We open a document on our computer, all set to begin, and that little cursor flashes at us, and we feel a little overwhelmed. Where do we begin?

Freewriting is a great place to start. Set a timer for fifteen minutes. During that time, you *have* to write, even if you write, "Ack! I can't think of what to write!" Your pen, or your fingers on the keyboard, must keep moving. Free-writing kick starts your creative flow. "When I have my students do freewrites in class, there are always lines they'll edit out later," Gore (2007: 69) writes. "But there's a coarseness and a truth they might never come to if they sat around waiting for just the right turn of phrase. In the dash to fill the page, the magic happens."

Rather than worry about the first sentence or the outline or the structure of your report, try just writing about what is on your mind regarding your research. Even if the words are "I need to write something about my research, which is about tattoo parlors." Okay, that's a start. Now write about something that happened at that tattoo parlor. Don't look at your notes, don't pull out your literature, just tell a story about the tattoo parlor. What does the tattoo parlor look like? What does it sound like? What does it smell like? Show me—your reader—what it is like inside of that tattoo parlor. Imagine that I've never been inside one, and put me there with your words.

Now that you have sketched out a description of the scene, go back to your data and identify one compelling incident from your field work. I know you have many, so just choose the first one you come across. We're trying to move your narrative from pure description of the environment to some action. What happened during this incident? Who was there? What did they say? What did they do? Show me what it would be like if I had observed the incident.

Give lots of detail about what happened. Maybe someone came in wanting a tattoo who was drunk, and he argued with the staff when they turned him away, and then he threw up all over the floor, and it smelled like vomit and margaritas. Maybe the artists practice tattooing their friends for free when the supervisor is gone. Maybe a client came in wanting a tattoo of her baby's face on her shoulder, but when the tattoo was finished, the baby looked demonic, and the client sobbed. Something happened in that tattoo parlor. Tell me about it.

Once you've written some action, explain to your reader what made this incident important in terms of the research. You can bring in your theoretical notes from your memos now. Maybe this incident exemplified a theme you noticed in your data. Perhaps the incident illustrates how people negotiate tattoo placement—whether the ink is visible in day-to-day life or hidden by clothing. Maybe the event illustrated some of the behind-the-scenes culture of tattoo artists. Perhaps you have a great commentary on the idea of permanence and the bodily. Here you are putting your scholarly spin—your interpretation—on the data.

Voila. You are on you way to have written up your research.

CHAPTER 27

WRITING AS PROCESS

All publications begin with words on the page. But they do not all end up where you expect. Writing is a process, just like field work, it's just a different sort of process. It unfolds in unexpected ways. The key is to find a process that works well for you.

The bulk of what I consider my good writing happens in coffee shops. I find it difficult to write at home. I'm too easily distracted—the dog wants to play, the kitchen is dirty, Facebook needs checking. I enjoy drinking good coffee when I write, nothing bitter, although I switch to decaf or sometimes herbal tea after one cup (too much caffeine and I start to feel scattered, which shows in my writing). I enjoy some background noise, provided it isn't too intrusive. I have a coffee shop noise threshold—too much and I become anxious. I don't like sitting next to people who talk loudly because I find myself eavesdropping on their conversation (hello, I am an ethnographer, kind of what we do). If that happens, I will move to another table. I can't write if I'm cold, so I usually bring a sweater, even in the summer (and I will turn up the thermostat when no one is watching—yes, I'm that person). If the weather is nice, I enjoy writing outside. I write by hand and prefer gel pens and high-quality paper, but I will write with whatever I have. I collect blank books and many of my friends support my writing habit with gifts of blank books and Starbucks cards at gift-giving occasions.

I type my manuscript into my computer at my office, editing my hand-written words as I type. I then print the draft, double spaced, single sided, stapled until it gets too thick, and I write on it by hand again, editing, adding more paragraphs here and there. It's a non-linear process that some of my writer friends argue is not terribly efficient, but it works for me. That is how I wrote the book you're reading now.

That is my process. You have to find a process that works for you. My friend Dona likes to wear fingerless gloves when she writes. When the gloves are on, she's a Writer. Her whole mindset changes to fit that role. Tom likes to go for a run before he sits down to write to clear his head. Some people find songs that fit the mood they are writing about and create a playlist to listen to as they type. One of the perks of being a writer is that we get some social allowance to be quirky in our art. So find what works for you and use it.

Scribbling out a document in the hours before it is due is probably not the best process. While a lot of students do this, it's a habit you should break now. We also don't have to write our masterpiece in one sitting (actually I would be shocked if anyone ever did—remember those shitty first drafts Lamott talked about?). Instead we write one word at a time, one sentence at a time. We step away from them. And later we come back and fiddle with them. Writing is a process, and like any process, you must allow yourself ample time to worth through the process in its entirety. As Goodall (2008: 38) said, "No one said thinking, or writing, was easy."

And like any process, the results may differ from what you expected when you began.

While working on my ethnography about natural gas drilling activism, I kept all of my notes and thoughts in one document on my computer, mainly to try to keep some sort of organizational control over them. The document kept getting longer and longer. As the research progressed, I found that my notes started to form three sections, one about specific health concerns, one about the participants and how they came to activism, and one about how they expressed their activism. I wrote headings for these three sections, and then subheadings, and began to better organize my notes in these sections.

I talked about the evolution of this document in my qualitative methods class one evening when my students asked about my writing process. I said I thought I would have three papers when I was finished.

"Maybe you're not writing papers," one of the students said. "Maybe you're writing a book."

I realized she was right. With a few modifications, that file eventually became a book. Those three sections became three chapters. I hadn't set out to write a book, I'd just written. Part of the idea of writing as inquiry is to let the work emerge and allow for the possibility that you may be surprised by the results.

CHAPTER 28

WRITING AS INQUIRY

Let's look more closely at that idea, of writing as inquiry. What I mean by that is that the act of writing itself is a way of thinking—and of knowing—about our work. Much of the analysis we perform on our data happens during the act of writing. Brilliant insights hit us midsentence. Laurel Richardson (2009), an advocate of writing as inquiry, writes:

> For the past twenty years or so, I have favored a reconceptualizing of qualitative research as not simply a 'mopping up' activity at the end of one's project, but as a method for finding theoretical ideas that were not apparent before the writing process. That is, writing is itself a method of inquiry that leads to new ideas.

Richardson argues that we should approach writing as both a creative and analytic process, that we allow ourselves the freedom to explore a multitude of forms and conventions (or lack thereof) that will allow both our unique voice and our *unique thinking* to emerge.

Likewise, Becker (1986: 17–18) argues that we should not wait until we are finished collecting data to begin our writing, because of the analytic process inherent in writing. "If you start writing early in your research," he said, "before you have all your data, for instance—you can begin cleaning up your thinking sooner. Writing a draft without data makes clearer what you would like to discuss and therefore what data you will have to get. Writing can thus shape your research design. This differs from the more common notion that you do your research first and then 'write it up.'" Indeed, "the presentation of reality is always a simultaneous construction of reality" Matt (2000: 327) reminds us.

The physical act of writing, whether by hand or on a computer, helps bring to light our subconscious thoughts about our research. Call it inspiration of the muses if you would like to be poetic about it, but sometimes thoughts you didn't even know you had spill out of you while you are writing. Sentences you hadn't thought to construct pour out of you onto the page. As Madden (2010: 153) writes, "Ethnographers do not need to feel they have all the answers, or to be fully reconciled to a certain form of interpretation, before they start writing up. These final resolutions are sometimes, in my experience, to be found in the process of writing." This is because of the connection between writing and thinking, because the act of writing is an act of thinking. "There is an interpretive element evident in the act of writing," Madden (2010: 156) adds, "the act of writing up causes us to reflect, to alter, to reconsider what we had in mind before we wrote 'up.'"

So while we are often accustomed to writing up at the end of our research process, if we accept the notion of writing as a form of inquiry, it behooves us to start writing early, to allow the act of writing to be part of our analytic practice, to allow writing to be a research method. Goodall (2008: 14) writes that "when we engage in writing or telling a story, we create alternative pathways to meaning that are imaginative *and* analytical; that are guided by a narrative (rather than a propositional) rationality; and that are relational— in the production of meaning, they connect the teller of the tale to the listener or reader of the story." Writing "*alters the way we think about* what we know and how we know it."

CHAPTER 29

DOING THE UNSTUCK

Writing as method is fine and dandy, but what should we do when we sit down to write and nothing comes out?

Writer's block is real. We all get it. I'm sorry to say that if you haven't yet experienced the crippling impotence of writer's block, you likely will at some point in your academic career.

"There are few experiences as depressing as that anxious barren state known as writer's block," Anne Lamott (2007: 176) writes, "where you sit starting at your blank page like a cadaver, feeling your mind congeal, feeling your talent run down your leg and into your sock."

Writer's block often happens when our creative well runs dry (Cameron, 1992). It's a signal that we need to practice some self-care and refill our well.

Imagine that we all have a well filled with creativity. We draw from that well continually, not only when we write, but in many different areas of our lives. Academics draw from our wells when we teach and present, when we design courses and lectures, when we write reports and emails, and all of the things we do that have nothing to do with writing up our research but require a creative bent. Anything that you do that requires creative energy draws from your well of resources.

That well must be refilled or it will run dry.

How do we fill the creative well?

Cameron (1992: 21) recommends taking yourself out on what she calls 'artist dates,' and we can use the same concept as ethnographers. To do this, you must identify what fills your creative well. What inspires you? What makes you feel alive? When I find myself depleted, I go for a hike. Being in nature recharges and grounds me. I also get inspired when I go to art museums (I'm particularly partial to modern art). Sometimes I need to crank up some music and sing. Sometimes I paint or draw—using a different form of creative energy can get me unstuck. Sometimes going to an academic conference gets ideas flowing. Or reading a novel.

"In filling the well," Cameron (1992: 21) writes, "think magic. Think delight. Think fun....Do what intrigues you, explore what interests you; think mystery, not mastery."

109

I tend to get in trouble when I don't take the time to refill my creative well. But feeling depleted doesn't help my career at all. We need to practice self-care. There is nothing selfish about taking time for yourself, about taking yourself on an artist date. Accept it as part of the writing up process and go play.

Many people say they want to be writers, when in fact what they want is *to have written*. They want lines on their vitas and to see their name on the covers of books. But being a writer and having written are not the same. Writing is work. Writing involves physically sitting down in a place and spilling words onto a page, and then crafting those words into a coherent, publishable form.

You won't always feel like writing. When I don't feel like writing, I can find a million distractions. I check my email and see what's happening over on Instagram. I walk the dog. I throw a load of clothes into the wash. I play some World of Warcraft. I cook something. Usually dessert. The problem is that all those things are not going to get my words out. None of them will result in my words in print and my name in lights. Don't wait until you feel like writing, because you may never feel like it. Write anyway. And don't find time. Make it.

I learned to schedule writing time from my friend (and prolific writer) Lisa Zottarelli. "When you are teaching, that time is sacred, right?" she asked me one day.

"Sacred?"

"Uninterruptible. You schedule around it. If someone wants to meet with you when you are scheduled to teach, you tell them, 'I'm teaching then,' and they understand that commitment. You don't go to meetings during your class. You have to be there, students count on you to be there and to be fully present. Why would you treat your writing any different? Because writing is just as important as teaching for academics. Writing time should be just as sacred."

That's not always easy for me. Because writing is a solo activity, no one but me holds me accountable. Students will complain if I don't show up to class. I will never have written if I don't show up to write.

But Lisa is correct. Writing is just as important in academia as teaching (if not more so). And I can teach my ass off but if I'm not writing I can kiss this job goodbye.

The same applies to graduate students. Graduate students often have inordinate demands on their time. They have to keep up with classwork to keep their professors happy. Oftentimes an assistantship means graduate students teach their own classes or that they help out their professors with teaching or research. They may hold a full-time job outside of their departments. Graduate students often have intimate relationships. A spouse or a partner not in graduate school may not fully understand the demands on their significant other's time. Many graduate students are at an age when their peers are getting married and having children. They may already have children themselves, and parenting is one of the most demanding drains on a person's time. And on top of all this, the faculty tell graduate students that they must publish or perish, that they have to begin filling their vitas with publications or they will have a terrible time finding a faculty position after graduation.

Writing is a solo activity. We need alone time to write. This is one area of our scholarly career where we are expected to be both independent and self-sufficient. We must find a way to do it and not use all our other commitments as reason not to write.

Fill the well if it is empty. And then sit in your chair and write.

INTEGRATING THE LITERATURE

Part of our task as academics is to situate our work within a larger scholarly conversation. One of the ways we do this is with our literature reviews.

In most scholarly writing, the literature review is a stand-alone section, or, in books, a unique chapter. Nonetheless, you should consider also integrating references to previous academic work throughout your own. Just as thick description provides weight for your analytic arguments, citations provide weight for your belonging in the larger academic field.

We should be aware of both the scholarly conversations surrounding our topics of interest and aware of how our work informs those conversations. We learn about those conversations through extensive reading. It's important that we follow citation strings backwards to understand how those conversations have evolved and who is doing the conversing. We can also learn about the current conversations when we attend academic conferences. This is not to say that you must only pursue hot topics in your field. But whatever work you are doing, someone else is, or has, written about some aspect of it.

By connecting your work with that of other scholars, you demonstrate the legitimacy of your place in the conversation about that subject. "Whether the research will count as knowledge or not depends on whether it is subsequently incorporated into other research reports as part of the literature review summarizing what we know about a given topic," Golden-Biddle and Locke (2007: 18) write. Integrating your own research into that scholarly conversation helps to legitimize your work as knowledge.

If you are anything like me, when undergoing a new research project you search for and print dozens if not hundreds of journal articles. You read them (or at least scan the introduction and maybe the conclusion), and maybe highlight or write on them. Hopefully you engaged the assistance of a good reference librarian to help you identify *all* of the literature in your particular academic conversation. A woman in my writing group brings a banker's box filled with printed journal articles and books to our writing sessions (perhaps not the best organization strategy, but it works well for her, and she's got quite the biceps from hauling that box around). I tend to keep them in stacks (that eventually collapse) all over my house. Luckily my spouse is also an academic, so he understands this mess and my need for him to leave it alone.

Organizing a literature review is not that different from analyzing qualitative data. Unfortunately, rather than integrating the literature into a cohesive narrative, many beginning scholars present a laundry list of previous studies to the reader. They summarize each article in a separate paragraph, and the literature review reads something an extended bibliography:

Ellis and Guffy (2012) wrote that...

Williams (2013) argued...

Ray (2011) said that...

This laundry-list approach shows that you read some things, but doesn't demonstrate your grasp of the larger arguments and nuances of the conversation. A good literature review synthesizes previous works and draws analytic conclusions from them (Savin-Baden & Major, 2013). I find that treating journal articles like data and organizing that data into themes (using our qualitative skills) the most effective way to develop an analytic literature review.

Let's look at an example. This is from an article I wrote about cancer cluster research (Gullion, 2014a: 404). In this paragraph, I draw on the literature about this type of research to specifically discuss data problems:

As in any other quantitative analysis, clusters can be found simply by chance (Drapper, 1997). This muddies the analysis, begging the question as to whether any given cluster has an identifiable cause. Oftentimes cases are double-counted by community members (Gavin & Catney, 2006), or old cases are counted in a present outbreak. There is often a lag time in the completeness and availability of registry data.

I go on to explain why this was the case in my own study. As you can see, the literature review is organized by theme rather than by individual studies conducted by other researchers. Rather than writing a paragraph about Drapper's study, followed by a paragraph about Gavin and Catney's study, I use their work to support a specific point that I want to get across—that there are data problems in cancer cluster research.

Another challenge many new scholars tell me they worry about is that they will pick a topic to research that's already been done. They worry about how they will contribute anything new to the discussion when so much has already been written, especially when they are supposed to do just that with their dissertations. I tell them to go conduct a quick literature search on cancer. Or tobacco. Or HIV. Researchers have written thousands of articles on these topics, and new research is published on them every week. But how is this possible? What's left to write? Hasn't it all been said by now?

No. And I will tell you why. Something will be unique in how you look at any problem, and that will emerge in your writing. I can give a class of twenty graduate students the same topic, the same set of journal articles to use in their literature reviews, and the same data set, and I will get back twenty unique papers. Why? Because we all come to any given problem with a unique standpoint, with our own way of seeing that problem.

Maybe what you have to say on a particular topic is not terribly profound. Ok, that's something you can work on. Remember, this is a career, not a one-shot task. With each piece you write, you build on your research agenda. You will enter the scholarly conversation about your topic. You will read more, engage more with other experts in your area of interest, and your thinking will become increasingly sophisticated. But whatever you say, it will be unique.

I once ran across a metaphor about writing that I adore. There are two ways that we can look at publishing. In one, we could say that the publishing world is a neighborhood with a set number of houses. Every published author resides in one of those houses. Once those houses are occupied, that's it, there's no more room. A lot of people look at publishing that way. They believe there are only a limited number of slots and that it is exceedingly difficult, if not impossible, to get one. And historically, that's kind of how academic publishing worked. There were a limited number of slots, of places to publish, and competition for those slots was fierce. But here's the thing—publishing is not a neighborhood of houses. It's an apartment complex, and when one complex is filled, *they build another one*. With the internet, self-publishing, e-journals, and so on, there are plenty of outlets for you to approach with your work. The key is to worry less about the topic you are writing about (i.e. cancer, tobacco) and more about how you write it. If you are passionate about your topic, that's enough. Write it well and you will find a publishing outlet.

And as a side note, remember that it is normal to approach more than one outlet before your work gets accepted. *Zen and the Art of Motorcycle Maintenance*, by Robert Pirsig, was rejected by 121 publishers before it was published. It sold five million copies.

WHAT TO CALL THIS THING?

I love writing clever titles. Unfortunately, librarians and tenure committees do not love clever titles. Why? Because they are difficult to search and to find in library databases. Other researchers need to stumble onto your work so that they can cite your ideas in their own work. Citation trails make careers, but while "God, Sex, and Cancer" is an amazing title (I wrote that one), HPV vaccine researchers are unlikely to open the file when they are working on their literature reviews (which is why my editor changed that title to the less amazing but more searchable Prejudicial Distribution of the HPV Vaccine).

Titles should tell the reader as succinctly as possible what the work is about. When writing a title for your work, give thought to the keywords that people might enter into a search engine. If you type "first responders influenza" into Google, the third link that comes up will be *October Birds: A Novel about Pandemic Influenza, Infection Control, and First Responders* (at least that's what came up when I wrote this paragraph). When I submitted the novel to the publisher, it was titled simply, October Birds. My series editor suggested adding the subtitle specifically to help other academics find the book when searching through the literature on their topics.

Think about your own literature searches. If you were searching for an article similar to what you are writing, what keywords would you use in the search engines? When I type "vaccine" into a Google Scholar search, I get 1.8 million hits. "HPV vaccine" gets me 60,000. Let's be honest here—I am not going to slog through 60,000 citations. Instead, I will try to find keywords that narrow down my search. Of course in doing so, I might miss articles that would be well suited for my literature review.

How many pages of citations do you read through before you decide you've seen enough? I ask this because the higher up you can get your own article in someone else's list, the more likely they are to see it and perhaps cite it. A descriptive title and some good keywords will help with that.

If you have a really great, clever title you can't bear to part with, consider the judicious use of the colon and write titles like reverse mullets: Party in the front and business in the back. God, Sex, and Cancer: Prejudicial Distribution of the HPV Vaccine would have incorporated both the clever title and the searchable keywords the editor wanted.

Also think hard about using special symbols or characters in your titles. The original title for *Fracking the Neighborhood* was *(In)Visibility in the Gas Field*. I thought it was a clever wordplay, an expression of becoming visible that social activists go though. My editor, however, explained that the parentheses are not always read the way you intend by search engines. Parenthesis are used differently by search engines and mean something explicit to the computer program. Removing the parentheses lost the meaning I wanted to convey, so we worked together on a title that captured what the book was about, improved search parameters, and improved marketability (plus the wordplay isn't terribly clear until you read the text and might turn some people off).

Academic writers don't typically think much about marketability and sales. We just haven't been trained to think of our ideas as commodities. But the truth is that marketability is an important piece of writing because we want to entice people to pick up our work and read it. Like it or not, the more people who cite our work, the more influential we are considered to be in our field.

THE PANIC ATTACK

You've finally written up your work. It's creative, well-developed. You follow a story arc, introduce intriguing characters living in a color-filled world. They encounter and overcome obstacles. You do it all with thick description and panache. You've inserted yourself into the scholarly conversation and found just the right title. Now it's time for the panic attack.

I don't advocate that you panic. On the contrary, I hope you don't. But this is the point where many writers have a momentary crisis, and if you feel that way yourself, know that it is perfectly normal, that you are not the first ethnographer to experience it, and that you will get through this.

Because I don't write linearly, I wrote the last chapter of this book before I wrote this one. I showed it to a colleague, who had some great feedback for me. She was the first person to see any part of this manuscript besides me. And right after I heard back from her, I entered the panic attack zone.

The book was almost finished—I would be sending it off to my series editor in less than two weeks. And I walked around my house feeling like I was going to vomit. I lay awake at night, staring into the darkness, worrying that everything I'd done was a waste, I wouldn't get tenure, and that people would laugh at me. I entered the zone Lamott (1994: 8–9) so eloquently describes:

> You may experience a jittery form of existential dread, considering the absolute meaninglessness of life and the fact that no one has ever really loved you; you may find yourself with a free-floating shame, and a hopelessness about your work, and the realization that you will have to throw out everything you've done so far and start from scratch. But you will not be able to do so. Because you suddenly understand that you are completely riddled with cancer.

Ethnography is not a quick research method. With fieldwork, analysis, and writing, we can take years to complete a project. We pour our lives into this work. What if no one likes it? *What if it sucks?*

Fear of rejection and fear of failure are normal responses to wrapping up our projects. If you are feeling that way, know that this is a stage in the process and push through it. Find yourself a counselor, a support group, or a drinking buddy if that is what you need. The only way the world will know your genius is if you make your work public. Hitting the "send" button to submit your work to a publisher can be one of the most terrifying experiences you will have as an academic. But it is also the only way you will have one of the most exhilarating—an acceptance letter.

FRAMING AND PUBLISHING

Gore (2007) advises, and I agree, that you publish before you are ready. That's not to say that you send out unfinished work, but that you get stuff out the door. You can spend all your life editing and reworking a piece. But that piece won't be published until you submit it somewhere. Sure, it may get rejected. That's fine, submit it someplace else.

"Your first published pieces will be incomplete and imperfect," Gore (2007: 122) writes. "Who cares? It's better to make a fool of yourself in front of a small audience than it is to steal from the world the light of your coming brilliance."

Where will you publish your work? The publishing venue itself will have a significant impact on the form and structure of your writing.

I typically write without consideration of where the work will be published. When I am satisfied with my document, I then search for possible outlets for the work and, if needed, edit as appropriate for that venue. My friend Lisa thinks I'm crazy—she doesn't write a word until she's identified where she wants to publish, and then writes specifically for that venue. And she's been successful with that approach. Try both approaches and see what works for you.

Wherever you decide to try to place your work, begin by looking through the venue's guidelines for authors. You can usually find these on the publications' websites and/or, for journals and magazines, near the front or back cover of each printed issue.

Read through the mission and scope of the publication. Does your work align with what the editor is trying to accomplish with that journal? If you have to stretch to make your work fit their philosophy, the answer is probably no. There are so many venues available—save yourself and the editor time by finding the right fit for your work.

Once you decide on a venue that seems to be a good fit, ensure that your piece clearly meets all of the publication's stylistic guidelines. For example, if the guidelines specify APA style, do not send in your article in Chicago style. Change the style throughout your piece first. Many articles are rejected outright not because the work isn't good, but because the guidelines were not followed.

The series editor of one of my books once told me that she received more than one thousand submissions for that particular series. As of this writing, that series contains eighteen published books. Reading a thousand books is a daunting prospect, to say the least. One way to cull that to a more manageable number is to eliminate all of the writers who did not follow the guidelines. Many editors will be reluctant to invest time in an author who won't follow directions.

In addition to reviewing the author's guidelines, review some sample work from that venue. For ease of discussion, I will use peer-reviewed journals as an example, but the same principle works for any outlet. When I am interested in publishing in a particular journal, especially if it is one that I do not read on a regular basis, I first look through the table of contents for the last few issues. I am interested in learning what kind of work the journal publishes *now*. Remember that a lot of journals have been in press for years, if not decades, but the mission and scope of the journal may change over time depending on the stance of the various editors. If I find that most of the articles in the journal involve statistical modeling and are highly quantitative, I know that this venue is probably not the best fit for the ethnographic work I do. Likewise for highly positivistic journals; the editor will probably not be interested in my philosophical orientation.

Make sure that you look at recent issues with the current editor. As editors change, the types of work the journal publishes may also change. I once chose to send a piece to a journal because several of my citations came from that publication. I used poetic analysis in the piece, and I was concerned about finding a venue open to the technique. The editor rejected the piece without sending it out for review, stating that the journal no longer published this type of work. The pieces that used poetic analysis published in the journal were done under the previous editor, which I should have noticed.

Once I gather from the mission and the table of contents that my work might fit well with that particular journal, I randomly pull two or three issues from the last couple of years and print off one or two articles from each. I don't care about the substance of the articles—I am looking at their underlying structure. I want to see whether there is a particular 'formula' for that journal. Do the pieces follow a similar outline? For example, do they all follow the introduction, theory, method, findings, discussion format? I want to understand how consistent this structure is. If it runs through all of the pieces I've pulled, I know I need to edit my own writing into that structure. If there is more room for variability, I don't need to worry as much about that.

I also read for the tone of the pieces. Are they in active or passive voice? Are they written in first or third person? If all the articles slant in a certain direction, I should follow that lead.

How much space do they devote to the specifics of method? If a significant portion of the articles talk about method, I should as well. If the authors dedicate only a paragraph or two to method, I need to do the same. The same goes for researcher reflexivity.

Some journals will explicitly not publish certain types of work, no matter how closely it fits the mission of the journal. For example, some editors will not consider autoethnography or poetry. Fine. Move on.

I say all this not to limit your creativity, but to ensure you have a realistic picture of how to get your work in print. Academic publishing takes an inordinately long time. As a rough average, you should anticipate that one year will pass between your first submission and the appearance of your article in print. If you have to resubmit rejected articles to new venues, that process gets longer and longer. Following the ideas above will increase your likelihood of being published.

Another issue to consider is page length and spatial limitations. Ethnographies are often book manuscripts for good reason—we need the space to present our compelling stories. Few journals will allow you to go over thirty pages total, and increasingly journals limit articles much further. Writing for journals should therefore be tight. Cut all superfluous text. Your work should be well edited. All words, all sentences, must have a specific purpose. This must also be balanced with the imperative to write an authentic representation. As such, in journal writing, you will likely present only part of the overall story.

If you are writing a book you will have more room to tell your tale. Anticipate that book publishing takes even longer than publishing a journal article. For many academic presses, production alone (that is the time of receipt of the final draft to print) takes about nine months or more. Make sure that you allot for time to press when you are thinking about the road to tenure—submit early and often.

As you read these instructions, you may have felt a bit stifled—why should you curtail your genius into some editor's format? If you would like to work to change the publishing industry, the place to do that is on editorial boards and by serving as a peer-reviewer. Develop your own book series or edited volume and solicit the types of work you would like to read more of and support. When editorial positions open up, serve in them. Many qualitative researchers complain that the more prestigious journals and book publishers in their field overly emphasize quantitative research. We need to work together to change that system. We do that by accepting positions of power. As an editorial board member, I have more power to shift the direction of the journal than I do as an author submitting my work there. And in the words of one of my favorite authors, Margaret Atwood (1986), when it comes to publishing, *"nolite te bastardes carborundorum."* Keep trying.

"Get used to publication," Gore (2007: 120) writes. "Get used to writing for strangers. Get used to the stupid things those strangers will tell you about your work. Get used to the awesomely heartening things they'll tell you." You must push past any fear of rejection or fear of criticism or you will never be published. It's that simple. And that complex. As I mentioned before, pushing that 'send' button to submit your work to a publisher is terrifying and exhilarating. But if you want your work published, you must write it and you must send it out.

REVISE AND RESUBMIT

Submitting your work to journals results in three possible outcomes: accept (sometimes with minor corrections needed), reject, or revise and resubmit.

If your work receives a revise and resubmit (also called an R&R), celebrate. Don't despair. This is (usually) a good thing. The journal is interested in your work, and the editor would like to publish it—after you work a bit more on the piece.

Typically, you will receive a letter from the editor along with specific comments from the reviewers. Read the comments and revise your paper accordingly. Of course some of the suggestions may not be practical—if, for example, if they ask you for data you don't have there may not be much you can do about it. Other comments will be straightforward, for example suggesting you reword confusing passages or include additional citations where more support is needed. When you resubmit, include a cover letter in which you detail how you specifically addressed each of the reviewer's comments.

There are admittedly a few occasions when you might choose to forgo on the revise and resubmit. This decision should not be taken lightly, as there is a good chance that you are walking away from a publication.

I once submitted a paper to one of the higher impact ethnography journals specifically because placing an article there would be great for my tenure bid. The article did not get great reviews, but the editor wrote that they liked the topic, and with some significant work on my part, the journal wanted to publish the piece. The work on my part included a complete dismantling of the piece and total rewrite. And the editor wanted me to use a different theoretical orientation than the one I actually used to guide my data collection. The reviewers offered plenty of suggestions as how to do this— ten pages of single-spaced suggestions. I should have walked away from it then, but I painstakingly rewrote the article. I resubmitted and received the not uncommon but very disheartening second R&R.

I was a bit miffed after all of the work I'd done to recraft the paper the way they wanted, but I became increasingly upset as I read through their latest round of comments. One reviewer wanted me to focus specifically on gender (that reviewer's area of expertise), changing the direction of the entire article based on a single quote from one of the female participants. While it was a good quote, I had a serious problem with this suggestions as issues of gender were not prominent in the study. The participant's comment, while interesting, in no way represented a theme in the research to build on. Indeed, while conducting the project I tried to focus on that aspect, but it proved fruitless. In this particular case, gender was not a core problem.

A second reviewer simply didn't like my findings. They were in contradiction with much of the previous work on the subject. I believed—and still do—that this was an important contribution of my work to the field, but the reviewer wanted me to rework the findings contrary to what I actually found.

Had I rewritten the piece incorporating this new round of changes, not only would I have not been authentic to my research, but I believe the changes would have been unethical. I chose not to pursue publication with that journal any further and successfully found another outlet.

Know before you submit anything that you will probably receive a revise and resubmit or a rejection on the article. Outright acceptance (or acceptance with minimal copyediting) does happen, but it is rare. Know also that if you do the work asked of you for an R&R, your chances of publication are quite high.

Do the work.

WRITING TO CONNECT,
WRITING FOR SOCIAL CHANGE

Social Change Piece

"The central dilemma of all efforts at witnessing. In the midst of a massacre, in the face of torture, in the eye of a hurricane, in the aftermath of an earthquake, or even, say, when the horror looms apparently more gently in memories that won't recede and so come pouring fourth in the late-night quiet of a kitchen, as a storyteller opens her heart to a story listener, recounting hurts that cut deep and raw into the gullies of the self, do you, the observer, stay behind the lens of the camera, switch on the tape recorder, keep pen in hand? Are there limits – of respect, piety, pathos – that should not be crossed, even to leave a record? But if you can't stop the horror, shouldn't you at least document it?" Behar (1996:2)

Denzin – write social science that matters

There's a famous photograph of a buzzard standing in wait near a starving, dying child. The child was [describe – crawling? CHECK, ADD DETAIL] The phogoraphrer made a choice, between documenting the horror and helping the child. [tell more about this]

Writing stories that matter. That give a glimpse into another social world. That spur understanding. Action. Justice. Social change.

Westbrook (2008:31): "The most convincingly written argument has no influence whatsoever if it does not reach those who can make things happen."

why do we write ethnography? I believe that most that man ethnographers would argue that we write to connect & write for social Δ.

112

127

Ethnography is challenging, time consuming work. So why are we drawn to ethnography as method? What compels us to traipse out into a field and write about what we find there?

Sure, some of it is sheer curiosity. But I also believe that many ethnographers are compelled to do this work for a higher purpose—we want not only to understand a particular phenomenon ourselves, but we also want to write to connect with others and write for social change.

Not long ago, the Chronicle of Higher Education printed an article titled, "How Sociologists Made Themselves Irrelevant," by Harvard sociologist Orlando Patterson (2014). As you can probably imagine, the title alone shook up a lot of people in my field. In the piece, Patterson argued that "sociologists have become distant spectators rather than shapers of policy," and that in our "efforts to keep ourselves academically pure, we've also become largely irrelevant in molding the most important social enterprises of our era."

Sociologist or not, I never want my work to be irrelevant, nor do I want the same to be said of yours. I don't want to be a distant spectator. I want to be an agent of social change.

Denzin (2003) argues that we should write social science that *matters*.

I approach ethnography as an ethical practice of social justice. I don't want to be accused of hiding in the so-called safety of the Ivory Tower (although admittedly, that Tower can be more of a cut-throat place than safe).

Szelenvi (2015), in "The Triple Crisis of Sociology," argues that sociologists have lost their political edge. He writes that while sociologists of the 1960s and 1970s actively promoted radical social change—even revolution—sociologists of today avoid such discussions. Formerly left-leaning sociologists have grown conservative; more concerned with our pensions than with changing the status quo.

This is not just a problem among sociologists, but across academia. The neoliberal turn threatens to push all of us back into positivistic research with evidence-based gold standards and technocratic decision-making.

Our strength as ethnographers is our ability to witness, and to retell stories. To help the standpoints of a variety of people be heard by those in positions of power to make real social changes. As Westbrook (2008: 31) notes, "The most convincingly written argument has no influence whatsoever if it does not reach those who can make things happen."

Yet too often students in the arts, humanities, and social sciences are trained to balk at social advocacy in the name of Science (with a capital S).

Like intergalactic explorers, we are taught to mind the Prime Directive—thou shalt not interfere in the natural development of a society. We are socialized to (attempt to) maintain objectivity and distance from our research subjects, and when we publish our findings in peer-reviewed research journals, we are done.

But at some point we must ask the question—so what? Why are we doing all this work? Where is the greater good? Yes, we help raise voices, but how do we broadcast those voices? How do we get those voices heard by a large audience?

Sadly, research into the readership of peer-reviewed journals indicates that most articles are read by less than 5 people. In a recent article on academic citations, Dahlia Remler (2014) noted that 32 percent of papers in social science journals are never cited by anyone else. While an increasing number of journals are becoming open access, most, particularly the most prestigious, still require either university or other research center affiliation (or a lot of cash) to access.

There is a great disconnect here. Knowledge is buried in our academic journals rather than being accessible to the people who could actually use it. There is a lack of translation from the academic to public realm.

Many of us are quick to offer commentary on social issues to our colleagues. Not long ago, my Facebook feed was filled with commentary about Ferguson and Baltimore and McKinney, Texas, peppered with phrases like 'structural inequality' and 'institutional racism.' As ethnographers, we are poised to move that discourse from armchair commentary to the public realm, using creative nonfiction to widen our audience.

Community programs are continually implemented without any ethnographic expertise included. And when *we* hear about the specifics of these programs, social scientists can often specify precisely why they will (and do) fail—we saw exactly how well those programs worked in our ethnographic research. We need to take a seat at the policy table. We need to share our knowledge with others.

As a reader of this text, you are a torchbearer for ethnography. How will you make sure that your work is not irrelevant? How will you engage the public with your work?

Herbert Gans (2002) wrote in the American Sociological Association newsletter, *Footnotes*, that more sociologists should engage in public intellectualism. That we should learn to translate academic publications to venues read by educated, lay readers. And really, this should not be just a call for sociologists, but for academics in general. Gans laments that so few sociologists have been 'appointed' by the media to be public intellectuals. But I will let you on to a secret—no one 'appoints' public intellectuals. To be a public intellectual, you must go do it. Write and submit OpEds to news outlets. Write and submit magazine articles or popular press books. Speak before city council and other legislative bodies. Collaborate on action research with organizations that need your help. The public won't reach out to you—you have to reach out to the public. For academic knowledge to become public knowledge, we have to overcome the taboo against talking to the public.

To be sure we must also contend with the expectations of our tenure and promotion guidelines. The glory for academics is *not* in public engagement but in peer-reviewed publication. If, to remain relevant, we decide that more public engagement is needed—and I believe we should—we also need to consider the weight of those activities in the promotion and tenure process.

I am also not arguing that *all* social science must be directed towards public engagement. Certainly there is a lot of work on methodology and theory and other topics that support our intellectual work that must continue. I do believe, however, that a lot of the research happening in universities could have significant social benefit and should be in the public realm for that purpose.

When we write ethnography for broad audiences, we can speak to the "so what" of our work. We can elicit action on the part of our reader. We can make a real differences in people's lives. We can write to both connect with others and to inspire social change.

I recently had the pleasure of watching Anne Harris perform her autoethnography, "Do It Like A Dude: Writing into / out of genderqueer visibility" (2015). In this piece, Harris transforms her raw emotional vulnerability into righteous power. Her work is a prime example of writing to connect and to inspire social change. When she finished her reading, I couldn't stop myself from hugging her close and saying "I love you!"

You should know that I am not a huggy person. I like my personal space and I tend to keep people out of my bubble. I also am not prone to professing my love to fellow presenters (even if they are my friends) during academic conference sessions. But I felt completely overwhelmed with emotion while listening to Harris' words, and that was the only response I had for her at the time.

Later that evening, she and I talked about how people respond to performance and autoethnography at academic conferences. "I wanted some feedback. What worked, what didn't," she told me. Instead, she got the ubiquitous, "that was powerful," and the (likely weird for her), "I love you."

I think oftentimes we don't have the language to express our responses to vulnerable work. Vulnerable writing elicits vulnerable responses in turn. Vulnerable writing also sticks with you long after you've finished reading a piece. Harris' words have stuck in my mind since that conference. I think about her and of all my other friends and colleagues who live with oppressions because of their expressions of gender. Harris was kind enough to let me share her piece with you:

Do It Like a Dude: Writing into / out of Genderqueer Visibility
by Anne Harris

Jose Munoz and before him Joan Nestle screamed back to the one persistent white straight male dominant culture they both seemed to find themselves trapped in that

WE ARE NOT LIKE YOU.

That queer desire is also persistent.

That silence equals death but speaking also sometimes equals death.

That homophobia and transphobia don't disappear post-Modern Family.

That Ellen has NOT made the world safe for all queers.

That Laverne Cox has NOT made the world welcoming for all gender outlaws and that

Visibility can be highly overrated.

That the queerest stuff is still found in the mainstreamiest places.

That Boylorn's (2013) blackgirl (one word) persists across subjectivities,

Here as boigirl (one word).

That a global epidemic of trans* youth suicide has replaced

The 'gay liberation movement' that I grew up in,

And

131

The world is still not safe for

Browngirls

Brownboys

Girlbois

Tranniegirls

Genderqueers

Pansexuals

Feminists

Postfeminists

Crips (Belluso, 2001)

Jews or

Muslims.

Why?

Why?

*

(breathe)

We can do it like the man

I can do it like a brother

Do it like a dude

Bong, bong, hey, hey, pour me a beer

No pretty drinks, I'm a guy out here

This line from the Jesse J song "Do It Like a Dude" makes me think about

two important notions in gender nonconforming communities and they both pivot on YOU, rather than on ME,

which right there is kind of fucked up. I mean,

The thing about being genderqueer in this world is that it's a social exercise, and so one of these things is supposedly good and one of them is BAD:

One is what some people call 'passing' (good)

And the other is 'being read' (bad).

In trans* terms,

Passing means for me that I have passed as a guy, that I have passed in the world as a guy which I feel like (on the inside) (some of the time).

If I am 'read' as a female, I have FAILED to pass as a guy,

I have been 'read' as a girl,

I have not achieved my trans* 'goal' of being 'seen' as my 'true' self.

Despite recent rejections of the term 'passing' in favour of the word 'being,' it remains in wide circulation even within trans* communities.

I do not believe in any of these markers, I am too old, too cynical and have fought too hard to believe there is one true self in here that I can BE or that I can SEE or know or fix.

If I were Boylorn I might say I am *girlboi* but I'm not Boylorn.

And Lauren Berlant says

"There is nothing more alienating than having your pleasures disputed by someone with a theory," (Berlant, 2012)

but I am not Berlant either

And I don't have a theory

I just have me. I have my blood and bones and flesh and history.

Some of which is a *herstory* thank you Joan Nestle it's true

And that herstory which I turned away from as a young gay woman

Because well because I guess see like it just sounded so

(beat)

Lesbian Herstory Archives, I mean. So uncool.

But now, well now, too many hurts, too much of our story untold, I've been alive too long and seen too much erasure of my own experience to care what it sounds like.

133

See, that archive is a thread, a cord,

A bastion against this tidal wave of that goddamn

One. Persistent. White. Male. Culture. That just keeps dominating no matter what we do. \\

The other thing that gets talked about a lot in the trans* world is hair.

And I'm switched on to hair, I am, from my many years in the lesbian movement, I am. But there's this thing about HAIR in the trans* world that kind of bugs me. It's like if you're working the M2F trans-ition, you don't want the hair that you've got. You gotta get rid of that hair to really PASS as a woman.

But if you're working the F2M trans-mobility and you want to pass as a guy? somehow hair is the thing.

Hair makes it real.

Hair makes me a guy.

But the thing is, twenty years ago when I was just an everyday run of the mill dyke, hair was the thing that made me a WOMAN. A gay woman. A lesbian woman. So apparently in one lifetime hair can denote being a transman OR being a queer woman but

I kinda like that. \\

(hashtag) #Boigirl

(hashtag) #girlboi

#hairygirl

#genderqueerhair

Kathleen Stewart says "The body is both the persistent site of self-recognition and the thing that will always betray you" (Stewart, 2005: 1024).

So here I am. Self-recognized and betrayed, all in one

And I don't hate it for that.

And I don't hate it for its hair, or its not-hair.

And I don't know how I want to be 'read' or when I might feel like 'passing.'

And if you recognise those terms as the selfsame terms that used to be used by people of colour moving through this

One. persistent. white. straight. male. culture.

You are right, because passing and being read has been a topic of some consideration—persistently—for most non-dominant folks for as long back as we can recall.

It's been a matter of survival.

Silence equals death, but so does being read. And sometimes, passing too equals a different kind of death.

Nestle says queerness is a 'persistent desire' & I must say I've often been praised for my persistence. \\

I am resilient, hard-working and stubborn.

These are good Protestant qualities in a mother or a homesteader, but not necessarily in a queer or a genderqueer person.

You don't get a lot of rewards in this life for being a persistent queer.

But I'm here to say that answering the call of desire \

in this sex-repressed and woman-choking culture \ is a victory.

It is a victory to admit and perform desire here.

Still.

Right now, in this room. /

When do we bring desire into our classrooms, our articles, our essays, our books?

How often do we encourage a persistent and relentless commitment to desire in our students?

How frightened are we still? //

We can do it like the man

I can do it like a brother

Do it like a dude

Bong, bong, hey, hey pour me a beer

No pretty drinks, I'm a guy out here

*

For masculine women or genderqueer girls, our masculinity is a sign of impudence or immaturity. Real women grow up, get curvy, soften.

Hard women are bitter, or under-developed.

Coming out as genderqueer feels a lot like when I came out as gay:

Somehow it either makes people really frustrated

or they try to reassure me by saying really homophobic, transphobic things like:

"You're not that masculine, my sister is more masculine than you and she has three kids!"

Like they used to say "You're not like most gay people. I usually don't get along with gay people, but you're different."

And that's supposed to be a COMPLIMENT? /

This world is not an easy place

And maybe its not even easy for middle-class straight white people, maybe its not.

But god I have spent so many untold countless daydreams wondering what it's like

Just for one day.

One. single. day.

to be straight and welcome in the world,

celebrated even, and move that easily through life.

Through people through culture through time.

That un-checked, that un-self-conscious, that entitled, that confident, that unreflexive.

I can tell you, it looks from here like

136

a beautiful long August afternoon

with a big fat summer iced tea

sitting on a porch where nobody's looking at me,

just me looking out at you,

a safe world, looking out seeing lots of me's out there,

looking out at the world through clear eyes.

Just everything in its place.

Time going by.

Sippin that tea.

Raising up my kids easy-like, confirmed by those around me, sharing the hard parts with family who have my back, because I can share my troubles, because everyone has the same troubles, and so someone can tell me its gonna be alright, and it is.

Because that is not what queer people or trans* people have.

And it's not alright.

Not in our bodies, our lives, our neighborhoods, our pants, our dresses, our families, or our days and nights. So we strive. We strive hard, PERSISTENTLY even, relentlessly, we strive to either fit in and do better than the next guy, to fit in BETTER than the average guy, or we strive to fit OUT, to be out and proud, to be queerer than the next girl. But there is seldom a middle ground. //

It's hard to find the middle ground without a tribe to keep your back.

Being read or passing, mmm.

For those of us in the queer diaspora, we never grew up in queer families,

we couldn't go home from the school bus bullies crying

and be cradled by queer mothers who wiped away our queer tears and taught us our proud queer histories and sent us off upstairs with a queer sandwich to play with our queer brothers and sisters to salve our wounds.

And if those queer families are finally arriving, the gladness of it takes time, as the sadness of those legacies, those Lesbian and Queer Herstories takes

137

time. And will it ever dissipate? Are we beyond Baltimore, beyond Ferguson, beyond Palestine? Have we progressed past queer youth bullying, or trans* youth suicides? Does that

One. Persistent. White. Straight. Male. Dominant. Culture. Recede?

Not yet.

Not for this hashtag girlboi oneword.

Not for me.

And I'm sorry if my anger makes you uncomfortable.

And I'm sorry if my genderqueer frustration after 35 years of lesbian compliance makes you weary for what might seem to you like queer hair-splitting.

And I'm sorry if you would rather think about other inequalities in the hierarchy of injustices in this world but you know what?

I don't care.

Cuz this is my margin, and I've been uncomfortable for so long, and I'm tired.

Tired of doing all the work.

And we got a right to rest.

And some of that work has to be done by you.

A nice dream. \\

A nice vision and lord knows we need dreams and visions to make any progress at all. But the problem is:

(and I'm gonna look to Stewart again because Stewart gives me a vision, and a dream, and some hope about feelings and bodies and love and desire):

Stewart schools me to remember that my complicated body is not separate from the social body, the body of YOU. She says my

"...lone body and the social body" are one, that together we are "the lived symptoms of the contradictions, conflicts, possibilities, and haunted sensibilities of pervasive forces" (Stewart, 2005: 1023).

That is why we must speak.

And I'm telling you I am living among some pervasive forces.

I live my truth among

Relentless productivity

Persistent racism

State-sanctioned violence against women and brown people

Cronyism among white academics and men that excludes everyone else:

EVERYONE else

And when the everyone-elses (one word) DO slip through the cracks of privilege,

we are allowed to be here only if we behave, and remember our place.

And when one of us succeeds, by sheer force of will and broken heartedness and stubborn refusal and GODDAMN PERSISTENCE

We are told that there is no more inequality and anger is unproductive.

So.

Let me invite you to consider the possibility that

Gender is just another straightjacket to freedom

& YOU TOO might not yet be free in YOUR gender, your desire, and

Our freedoms are inter-dependent.

So let me celebrate my beautiful girlboi self if I want to without

Patronizing me, or exoticisng me or asking if you can see my dick.

I mean, really. True story.

Every day I perform my version of gender

I often go unseen, unremarked

While at the same time being just different enough to keep you on edge.

They say we live in a visual culture these days and we do we surely do

139

But for this girlboi, visual is only as visual as I make it.

I resist taking T and growing a beard and being that newly-visible newly-intelligible trans*man you think you know.

I'm not him.

And I will not let you touch my dick.

And I do not have to help you understand

Or explain what it means to me

Or how I got here.

And all of it's real.

all of its me.

#Girlboi one word.

And if you are so eager to say "Go ahead, be masculine, love yourself honey, don't compromise!"

Just take a minute. Check yourself and

Think about how masculine women are treated in this world.

How welcome in the change room, the bathroom, the dinner party, the conference?

How many of you have a genderqueer 'handbag' that you fetishize at your parties and dance clubs, like fag hags or your gay boyfriend on your arm?

There is no such thing as a 'butch-hag' for a reason. \

We're not like that.

Not as good in crowds. Not as much fun.

So think about what you are encouraging us to do,

So cavalier.

There is a price for being different in this world, make no mistake.

There is still a very high price.

So we don't need dicks to do it like a dude, we just need moxy.

Because like Jessie J says,

We CAN do it like the man

Or do it like a brother

Or Do it like a dude

I can pass or I can be read.

Depending on what I feel, what I wear, how I walk:

I know how to play.

And for me, the play's the thing (as Shakespeare said, another very queer interventionist)—

The play IS the thing

Not drawing lines in the sand and forcing me—and you—to choose sides.

Cuz that's a too-tight dress or a dress suit for hire, but

Desire—to me—is the ultimate one size fits all.

Without needing to deficit frame me up like mainstream culture loves to do:

Why do we cling to terms like "Gender-non-conforming" //

What about gender expansive?

What is it in our persistent western white male culture that demonizes everything it doesn't understand?

Our time here is short.

Our joys are precious and few.

Desire is a gift not to be squandered

Desire and the body, gender and sexuality—what beautiful gifts we have found ourselves in.

Imagine, like Samantha in the movie *Her* to have desire with NO body.

How truly blessed we are. and Me?

I'm doubly-blessed.

Boigirlblessed (one word).

While listening to Harris' piece, I found myself in a state of tension, between feeling her rage and power (and wanting to shout, "you go girl, right on, it's the hair!"), and knowing that I am a heterosexual, married, white women, with two children (a boy and a girl), a dog, a cat, two cars, and a mortgage. I am the epitome of the conservative ideal, of the reified nuclear family, with all the privileges that go along with that. And I kept thinking, why me? Why should I have privileges because of my expression of gender while Harris is oppressed because of hers? And I kept thinking: This. Is. Wrong. And I kept thinking: This cannot continue. I will not allow this to continue.

How will I move from feeling to action? I don't always know what that looks like, and I'm working on that. I'm sharing her piece here so you can read it, and I hope you are as moved by it as I am. I'm looking for opportunities to make social change so that Harris and others don't have to carry this burden alone—I want them to know that my hands are here to help hold this and that my back is strong.

This is the power of vulnerable writing. This is how you connect with other people. And this is how your writing changes the world.
Denzin (2003) implores us: Write social science that matters.

There's a Pulitzer-prize winning photograph of a buzzard standing in wait near a starving, dying child. The child struggled to get to a food distribution center, dragging her body through the dirt with emaciated limbs, her ribs each visible, her belly swollen with starvation. The photographer, South African photojournalist Kevin Carter, committed suicide the year after he received the award (NPR, 2006). Carter found himself caught in the horror between documenting the atrocity and intervening to save the child. He opted to take the photograph. This is a quote from Carter, from "The Death of Kevin Carter," a film about his work produced after his suicide:

> It may be difficult for people to understand, but as a photojournalist, my first instinct was to make the photograph. As soon as that job was done and the child moved on, I felt completely devastated. I think I tried to pray; I talked to God to assure Him that if He got me out of this place I would change my life. (NPR, 2006)

The director of the film told NPR:

> They are gut-wrenching pictures. I mean, we're talking about extreme degrees of violence, people being burned alive, being hacked to death. These photojournalists were not afraid of being very close to the violence that they were witnessing. And in some cases, I think these

photographers were willing to risk injury or death to get a prize-winning picture. I mean, they were driven to make compelling pictures partly because of their own ego as photo journalists, but also because they had a great sense of mission and they knew that these photographs had the power to change public policy and public awareness of what was happening in their country.

Like photojournalists, ethnographers are witnesses to culture, to history. And Carter's story is "the central dilemma of all efforts at witnessing. In the midst of a massacre, in the face of torture, in the eye of a hurricane, in the aftermath of an earthquake, or even, say, when the horror looms apparently more gently in memories that won't recede and so come pouring fourth in the late-night quiet of a kitchen, as a storyteller opens her heart to a story listener, recounting hurts that cut deep and raw into the gullies of the self, do you, the observer, stay behind the lens of the camera, switch on the tape recorder, keep pen in hand? Are there limits—of respect, piety, pathos— that should not be crossed, even to leave a record? But if you can't stop the horror, shouldn't you at least document it?" Behar (1996: 2) asks.

We must ask ourselves the same. What is the purpose of writing ethnography? I'd like to think it is to change the world. To connect with others. To make things better.

Ethnographers are the witnesses. These are our stories.

And the world is ready to read yours.

ETHNOGRAPHIC INSPIRATION

Auyero, J., & Swistun, D, A. (2009). *Flammable: Environmental suffering in an Argentine Shantytown*. New York, NY: Oxford University Press.

An exploration into coping mechanisms of people living in a highly contaminated shantytown in Argentina, one which health officials there have declared to be unfit for human residence.

Bourgois, P., & Schonberg, J. (2009). *Righteous Dopefiend*. Berkeley, CA: University of California Press.

A compelling work on homeless heroin uses in San Francisco.

Duneier, M. (2000). *Sidewalk*. New York, NY: Farrar, Straus and Giroux.

An examination of the informal economy of street vendors in New York.

Erikson, K. T. (1976). *Everything in its path: Destruction of community in the Buffalo Creek flood*. New York, NY: Simon and Schuster.

A classic study on the impact of disaster on a community.

Fadiman, A. (1997). *The spirit catches you and you fall down: A Hmong child, her American doctors, and the collision of two cultures*. New York, NY: Farrar, Straus and Giroux.

A heartbreaking account a Hmong immigrant family's experience with the US healthcare system and their epileptic child.

Kohn, E. (2013). *How forests think: Toward an anthropology beyond the human*. Berkeley, CA: University of California Press.

An ethnography that explores the mutual entanglements of the human and nonhuman in the Ecuadorian Amazon.

Minge, J. M., & Zimmerman, A. L. (2013). *Concrete and dust: Mapping the sexual terrains of Los Angeles*. New York, NY: Routledge.

An arts-based ethnographic account of sexual identity and sexual agency in Hollywood.

Rivera-Servera, R. H. (2012). *Performing Queer Latinadad: Dance sexuality, politics*. Ann Arbor, MI: The University of Michigan Press.

A multiple award-winning ethnographic account of performance in Latina/o queer public culture.

Saldanha, A. (2007). *Psychedelic White: Goa trance and the viscosity of race*. Minneapolis, MN: University of Minnesota Press.

Through a study of rave culture in India, this ethnography presents a Deleuzian conceptualization of race.

Stewart, K. (1996). *A space on the side of the road: Cultural poetics in an "Other" America*. Princeton, NJ: Princeton University Press.

An intriguing insight into the culture and landscape of the coal-mining area of Appalachia.

Valentine, D. (2007). *Imagining transgender: An ethnography of a category*. Durham, NC: Duke University Press.

This ethnography explores the emergence and embracing of transgender as a signifier of identity.

Wacquant, L. (2004). *Body and soul: Notebooks of an apprentice boxer.* New York, NY: Oxford University Press.

A three-year study of a boxing gym in Chicago.

Wong, Y. (2010). *Choreographing Asian America.* Middletown, CT: Wesleyan University Press.

A dance ethnography that explores the influence of Orientalist appropriation in US modern dance.

ADDITIONAL WRITING GUIDES

Becker, H. S. (1986). *Writing for social scientists: How to start and finish your thesis, book, or article*. Chicago, IL: University of Chicago Press.

Behar, R. (1996). *The vulnerable observer: Anthropology that breaks your heart*. Boston, MA: Beacon Press.

Cameron, J. (1991). *The artist's way: A spiritual path to higher creativity*. New York, NY: Putnam.

Golden-Biddle, K., & Locke, K. (2007). *Composing qualitative research* (2nd ed.). Thousand Oaks, CA: Sage.

Goodall, H. L. (2008). *Writing qualitative inquiry: Self, stories, and academic life*. Walnut Creek, CA: Left Coast Press.

Gore, A. (2007). *How to become a famous writer before you're dead: Your words in print and your name in lights*. New York, NY: Three Rivers Press.

King, S. (2000). *On writing: A memoir of the craft*. New York, NY: Pocket Books.

Lamott, A. (1994). *Bird by bird: Some instructions on writing and life*. New York, NY: Anchor Books.

Narayan, K. (2012). *Alive in the writing: Crafting ethnography in the company of Chekhov*. Chicago, IL: The University of Chicago Press.

Richardson, L. (1997). *Fields of play: Constructing an academic life*. New Brunswick, NJ: Rutgers University Press.

REFERENCES

Atwood, M. (1986). *The handmaid's tale*. New York, NY: Anchor Books.

Barker-Ruchti, N., & Tinning, R. (2010). Foucault in Leotards: Corporeal discipline in women's artistic gymnastics. *Sociology of Sport Journal, 27*, 229–250.

Becker, H. S. (1986). *Writing for social scientists: How to start and finish your thesis, book, or article*. Chicago, IL: University of Chicago Press.

Behar, R. (1996). *The vulnerable observer: Anthropology that breaks your heart*. Boston, MA: Beacon Press.

Belluso, J. (2001). *Body of bourne (A play)*. New York, NY: Playscripts.

Berlant, L. (2012). *Love/Desire*. London, England: Punctum Books.

Boylorn, R. M. (2013). Blackgirl blogs, auto/ethnography, and crunk feminism. *Liminalities: A Journal of Performance Studies, 9*(2), 73–82.

Cameron, J. (1991). *The artist's way: A spiritual path to higher creativity*. New York, NY: Putnam.

Colosi, R. (2010). *Dirty dancing? An ethnography of lap dancing*. New York, NY: Routledge.

DasGupta, S. (2014). Narrative medicine, narrative humility. *Creative Nonfiction, 52*, 6.

Dennis, B. (2010). Ethical delimmas in the field: The complex nature of doing education ethnography. *Ethnography in Education, 5*(2), 123–127.

Denzin, N. (2003). *Performance ethnography: Critical pedagogy and the politics of culture*. Thousand Oaks, CA: Sage.

Duneier, M. (2011). How not to lie with ethnography. *Sociological Methodology, 41*(1), 1–11.

Ellis, C. (2009). *Revision: Autoethnographic reflections on life and work*. Walnut Creek, CA: Left Coast Press.

Flyvbjerg, B. (2001). *Making social science matter: Why social inquiry fails and how it can succeed again* (Steven Sampson, Trans.). New York, NY: Cambridge University Press.

Frank, C. R. (2004). Ethnography for teacher education. *Journal of Teacher Education, 55*(3), 269–283.

Gans, H. (2002). More of us should become public sociologists. *Footnotes*. Retrieved July 28, 2015, from www.asanet.org/Footnotes/julyaug02/fn10.html

Golden-Biddle, K., & Locke, K. (2007). *Composing qualitative research* (2nd ed.). Thousand Oaks, CA: Sage.

Goodall, H. L. (2008). *Writing qualitative inquiry: Self, stories, and academic life*. Walnut Creek, CA: Left Coast Press.

Greetz, C. (1973). Thick description: Toward an interpretive theory of culture. In C. Greetz (Ed.), *The interpretation of cultures: Selected essays*. New York, NY: Basic Books.

Gore, A. (2007). *How to become a famous writer before you're dead: Your words in print and your name in lights*. New York, NY: Three Rivers Press.

Gullion, G., & Gullion, J. S. (2015). *Actor network theory and Somalian piracy*. American Criminal Justice Society annual conference, Orlando, FL.

Gullion, J. S. (2014a). This toxic material. *International Review of Qualitative Research, 7*(4), 401–420.

Gullion, J. S. (2014b). *Cancer/Environment Rhizomes*. International Congress of Qualitative Inquiry annual conference, Champaign, IL.

REFERENCES

Gullion, J. S. (2015). *Fracking the neighborhood: Reluctant activists and natural gas drilling.* Cambridge, MA: The MIT Press.

Gullion, J. S., & Ellis, E. G. (2013). A pedagogical approach to action research. *Journal of Applied Social Science, 8*(1), 61–72.

Hart, J. (2011). *Storycraft: The complete guide to writing narrative nonfiction.* Chicago, IL: University of Chicago Press.

King, S. (2000). *On writing: A memoir of the craft.* New York, NY: Pocket Books.

Kusiak, P. (2008). Sociocultural expertise and the military: Beyond the controversy. *Military Review, 88*(6), 65–76.

Lamott, A. (1994). *Bird by bird: Some instructions on writing and life.* New York, NY: Anchor Books.

Leavy, P. (2015). *Low-fat love, expanded anniversary edition.* Rotterdam, The Netherlands: Sense Publishers.

LeCompte, M. D., & Schensul, J. J. (2013). *Analysis and interpretation of ethnographic data: A mixed methods approach* (2nd ed.). New York, NY: AltaMira Press.

Madden, R. (2010). *Being ethnographic: A guide to the theory and practice of ethnography.* Los Angeles, CA: Sage.

Malinsky, L., Dubois, R., & Jacquest, D. (2010). Building scholarship capacity and transforming nurse educator's practice through institutional ethnography. *International Journal of Nursing Education Scholarship, 7*(1), 1–12.

Matt, E. (2004). The presentation of qualitative research. In U. Flick, E. von Kardoff, & I. Steinke (Eds.), A *companion to qualitative research* (B. Jenner, Trans., pp. 326–330). London, England: Sage.

Narayan, K. (2012). *Alive in the writing: Crafting ethnography in the company of Chekhov.* Chicago, IL: The University of Chicago Press.

Nardi, B. A. (2010). *My life as a night elf priest: An anthropological account of World of Warcraft.* Ann Arbor, MI: University of Michigan Press.

National Public Radio (NPR). (2006). *A pulitzer-winning photographer's suicide.* Retrieved from http://www.npr.org/templates/transcript/transcript.php?storyId=5241442

Patterson, O. (2014). How sociologists made themselves irrelevant. *Chronicle of Higher Education.* Retrieved July 28, 2015, from http://chronicle.com/article/How-Sociologists-Made/150249/

Paulson, S. (2011). The use of ethnography and narrative interviews in a study of 'Cultures of Dance'. *Journal of Health Psychology, 16*(1), 148–157.

Pine, A. (2013). Revolution as care plan: Ethnography, nursing, and somatic solidarity in Honduras. *Social Science and Medicine, 99*, 143–152.

Remler, D. (2014). *Are 90% of academic papers really never cited? Reviewing the literature on academic citations.* Retrieved July 28, 2015, from http://blogs.lse.ac.uk/impactofsocialsciences/2014/04/23/academic-papers-citation-rates-remler/

Richardson, L. (1997). *Fields of play: Constructing an academic life.* New Brunswick, NJ: Rutgers University Press.

Richardson, L. (2009). Writing theory in(to) *Last Writes.* In A. J. Puddephatt, W. Shaffir, & S. W. Kleinknocht (Eds.), *Ethnographies revisited: Constructing theory in the field.* London, England: Routledge.

Saldaña, J. (2011). *Fundamentals of qualitative research.* New York, NY: Oxford University Press.

Savin-Baden, M., & Major, C. H. (2013). *Qualitative research: The essential guide to theory and practice*. New York, NY: Routledge.

Simmons, D. (2011). The role of ethnography in STI and HIV/AIDS education and promotion with traditional healers in Zimbabwe. *Health Promotion International, 26*(4), 476–483.

Smith, L. T. (2012). *Decolonizing methodologies: Research and indigenous peoples* (2nd ed.). London, England: Zed Books.

Sommerville, M. (2013). *Water in a dry land: Place learning through art and story*. New York, NY: Routledge.

Sparkes, A. C. (2002). Autoethnography: Self-indulgence or something more? In A. P. Bochner & C. Ellis (Eds.), *Ethnographically speaking: Autoethnography, literature, and aesthetics* (pp. 209–232). Walnut Creek, CA: AltaMira Press.

Stewart, K. (2005). Cultural poesis: The generativity of emergent things. In N. Denzin & Y. Lincoln (Eds.), *Handbook of qualitative research* (pp. 1015–1030). London, England: Sage.

Szelenvin, I. (2015). The triple crisis of sociology. *Contexts*. Retrieved July 28, 2015, from http://contexts.org/blog/the-triple-crisis-of-sociology/

Van Maanen, J. (2011). *Tales of the field* (2nd ed.). Chicago, IL: University of Chicago Press.

Westbrook, D. A. (2008). *Navigators of the contemporary: Why ethnography matters*. Chicago, IL: University of Chicago Press.

Whyte, L. A., & Buckner, K. (2001). An ethnography of a neighborhood café: Informality, table arrangements, and background noise. *Journal of Mundane Behavior, 2*(2), 195–232.

Williamson, S., Twelvetree, T., Thompson, J., & Beaver, K. (2012). An ethnographic study exploring the role of ward-based advanced nurse practitioners in an acute medical setting. *Journal of Advanced Nurse Practitioners, 68*(7), 1579–1588.

ABOUT THE AUTHOR

Jessica Smartt Gullion, PhD, is Assistant Professor of Sociology and Affiliate Faculty of Women's Studies at Texas Woman's University, where she teaches a variety of courses on qualitative research methods and medical and environmental sociology.

She has published more than 30 peer-reviewed journal articles and book chapters. Her writing has appeared in such journals as the *International Review of Qualitative Research*, the *Journal of Applied Social Science*, and *Qualitative Inquiry*.

Dr Gullion's other books include *Fracking the Neighborhood: Reluctant Activists and Natural Gas Drilling* (The MIT Press, 2015) and *October Birds: A Novel about Pandemic Influenza, Infection Control, and First Responders*, which is part of Sense Publishers' award-winning Social Fictions series (2014).

Her essays and Op-Eds have appeared in a variety of outlets, including *Newsweek*, *The Conversation*, *Alternet*, and *Inside Higher Ed*, and she is regularly quoted by national media.

Lightning Source UK Ltd.
Milton Keynes UK
UKOW06f1049210116

266832UK00001B/14/P